Scared Straight

Why It's So Hard to Accept Gay People
And Why It's So Hard to Be Human

Robert N. Minor, Ph.D.

A CONSORTIUM BUILDING:

Published by HumanityWorks!
4047 Botanical Avenue, Suite 200
St. Louis, MO 63110-3905
1-314-771-1908, Humanitywks@aol.com

Publisher's Cataloging-in-Publication
(Provided by Quality Books, Inc.)

Minor, Robert Neil, 1945-
    Scared Straight : why it's so hard to accept gay people and why
it's so hard to be human / Robert N. Minor. – 1st ed.
    p. cm.
    Includes bibliographical references.
    LCCN: 2001089450
    ISBN: 0-9709581-0-2

    1. Homosexuality–United States. 2. Gays–United States–Social
conditions. 3. Sex role–United States. 4. Gay and lesbian studies.
I. Title.

HQ76.25.M56 2001   306.76'6
                          QBI01-200459

First Printing, June, 2001
Second Printing, November, 2001

Cover design and book layout by Gary Rockhold.

CONTENTS

INTRODUCTION

"Scared Straight." Both words are crucial. This book argues that fear (phobia), being scared, is even more important than misinformation about ourselves and others. Fear is at the heart of the problems our culture has with the full acceptance of gay people, and it is also why all of us have problems getting in touch with our humanity. "Straight" names that problem. But "straight" does not mean heterosexual. It means something much more, a burden that we all carry in the form of how we are expected to live in our society.

The two subtitles — "Why It's So Hard to Accept Gay People" and "Why It's So Hard to Be Human" — are inextricably linked. This book argues that none of us, regardless of sexual orientation, will be able to live as human beings until we are able to fully accept transgendered and bisexual people and lesbians and gay men as invaluable gifts of our common humanity. The fact is, getting in touch with our humanity, no matter what our sexual orientation, is tied to doing the fear work we all need to do so that all of us can embrace gay people. And that means that, by doing their own fear work, gay people themselves will find a greater self-acceptance.*

*I use the term "gay" in two senses which I hope are obvious from the context. First, I use "gay" and "non-heterosexuals" as short-hand to refer to people who do not identify their sexual orientation as heterosexual. When I am referring only to gay men,

This book grows out of the expressed desires of the people who have attended my workshops and lectures on "Understanding Homophobia" or on sexuality and gender for the last ten years. They have been newcomers to the topic as well as seasoned veterans and activists who were looking for something more than the usual analyses, something that made sense regarding the difficulty of dealing with, and the apparent cultural "stuckness" over, this issue. They asked for something further to read and consider as they contemplated their next step toward healing our culture's diseases of sexual confusion, gender rigidity, homophobia, and the oppression of transgendered and bisexual people and gay men and lesbians. They were PFLAG members, religious leaders, activists, teachers, professors, social workers, seminary, college and high school students, heterosexual, bisexual, homosexual and uncertain-sexual people, upper, middle and working class people, and others who found something in my presentations that made sense to them and helped them progress in their lives, work, loves, and leadership.

Like those presentations, the value of what is found here is whether it makes sense to you and works for you. If it does, it is yours to help you move toward your humanity as you define it for yourself. If it doesn't all fit, take what helps and let the rest go. I put this forward because many have found it a break-through in their understanding, something helpful in relating to their own experiences, and something that touches what they already somehow knew was true. I don't suggest that this is the only way to understand the issues of the title of the book, but I think it is an essential key to where we are as we begin the twenty-first century.

I will say "gay men." Second, beginning in chapter seven I refer to the "gay" role that society attempts to condition non-heterosexuals to live in response to the dominant "straight role." At times I consciously choose to write out the full "transgendered and bisexual people and lesbians and gay men," so that we continue to remember that we are talking about people who have often been unmentioned and for whom the silence itself has hurt. Though I do not deal with it here, I would also like to assume there is a category such as "uncertain-sexual" because I believe a healthy society would allow uncertainty and ambiguity. And I fully recognize that no matter what our self-identified sexual orientation, we fear and even deny such ambiguity.

I would like to believe that our society has already moved beyond what this book says is the current conditioning. There is no question to me that we have made progress in our general cultural consciousness. There may be some people who feel that we have moved on. I often find these to be people who have "made it" financially or professionally in the system.

Yet again and again as I travel around the country I find that this book is still crucial. I read the news stories which tell of the religious, legal, political, and social backlash against the progress that sexual minorities have made. I speak to high school and university students around the country who when hearing these ideas rather than responding that this no longer is their experience tell stories of how this is still hopelessly "so true." I stand in a Metro station in downtown Washington, DC and hear the same slurs against "fags" that I hear everywhere else, and so I move in to stand close to those who are using them so they know someone is listening who might object. I hear the fear of clergy who know this is right and discrimination is wrong, but might lose their pulpits and congregations if they pushed this issue. I speak to parents of gay men, lesbians, transgendered and bisexual people and hear their pain as they come to accept, value, and work to end discrimination they and their children are still experiencing. I sit in the debates of churches who want to be affirming and yet worry that "We might become a gay church," indicating that "gay" is still a negative thing for them. I listen to gay people as they argue with each other over leadership, tactics, money, sex, gender issues, strategies, and how to and whether not to assimilate, and I see it deplete their energy. And I see members of the gay community still acting out a victim role and living in shame over the fact that they are sexual beings who love their same sex, even translating that shame into political strategies which hide same-sex sexuality.

On top of all this, even after the decades of the second wave of a women's movement which has taught us much, and a shorter men's movement in which men were trying to break out of conditioned gender patterns, I still see a nation obsessed with maintaining gender roles and continuing to promote a national foreign policy based on conditioned ideas of male honor and shame. I see women leaders who have often tried to make it in this straight, masculine-defined society continuing to be misrepresented in mainstream media and others frustrated and burned out over a sense of being bogged down. I see men's groups struggling to know why they exist and where to go next. I see therapists who are still trying to help people cope with a system that is profit-oriented and coping-oriented, not human-oriented or healing-oriented. We still have quite a way to go to crack the hold of a dysfunctional masculinity on the world and the corresponding feminine gender role which is still one telling women that the answer to their problems is to respond to male conditioning.

I am convinced that issues of gender roles, what is masculinity, what is femininity, go hand in hand with the acceptance of people who do not identify as heterosexual. And I am convinced that these issues are deeper, and more destructive to our humanity, than many of us have imagined. These are not just theoretical questions or surface issues easily educated away, but deeply inculcated elements of the way we are accustomed to see things. Hence the two subtitles of this book; we will not be in touch with what it is to be human as long as we cannot accept, affirm, and value transgendered and bisexual people and lesbians and gay men.

Many people and experiences have influenced me in writing this book. Actually the readings at the end of each chapter were discovered subsequent to the ideas here, but they are listed to encourage further study and personal growth and to allow me to affirm something of the breadth of the community in which I write and work. I have also read many of the conservative responses to these writings and found that those I recommend stand-up against the critics who don't want to change the structure of things.

Those who have attended my workshops have added so much to my understanding. What is exciting is that they have come with such a variety of backgrounds. I remember an early workshop for the Methodist parishes in extreme northern Kansas, held in the small town of Bern which is up near the Kansas-Nebraska border. Those thirty people who committed a half-day to this work were the first to teach me that all over the country, in places which seem to be "the middle of nowhere" to city folk, there are people, yes even religious people, who know that something is wrong with the current dominant rhetoric of anti-gay religious and political extremists. The challenge is that no one is speaking with them to affirm their intuitive suspicions and to give them the chance to grow on the issue of understanding and dismantling homophobia.

Since that experience, I have understood what many settled leaders in the big cities on the coasts seem to miss — there is more intelligence and anxious but hopeful waiting out there than we can imagine. The stories of people's lives I hear in these workshops and in response to lectures affirm this work, teach me much, and feed my hope.

Chapter seven is a narrative form of some of the work I facilitate in workshops for transgendered and bisexual people and lesbians and gay men on the next step after "coming out." It is meant to help us understand the propensity people who have been victimized by our culture have to live the victim role in which society wants them stuck. It is important for me to say here that I do not want to "blame the victim" for the real oppression that takes place daily in our culture and is often ignored by the mainstream. Yet, many gay people have responded that the workshop on moving out of the "victim role" that our culture expects them to live, is a powerful process in understanding what is going on — particularly if they have tried to be activists — and in seeing their place in gaining back their power and perspective.

Nothing in this book is meant to blame anyone. I am convinced that there are no human enemies. People tend to be doing the best they can, given their own personal past hurts and the pressures of a dysfunctional cultural and social system. The enemy to be changed is the system that humans have set up and continue to worship. I have yet to meet a human being that is violent and hateful who is not telling me by her or his actions how she or he was brought up. I suspect this is what was meant by a disciple of Jesus of Nazareth when he wrote: "We wrestle not against flesh and blood but against principalities and powers. . . ."

I owe my initial inspiration to an international men's workshop leader, Charlie Kreiner. His fingerprints are all over this book. Yet I do not want him to be held responsible for what is here, because this is my version, interpreted, selected, expanded, adjusted, and enlightened by the people and writers I have since encountered. Much of what I have said here has been said before in scattered books and articles by feminist writers, most of whom are women. As you will no doubt understand by the time you have read this book, however, given the continuing presence of sexism in our culture, when a white, male says the same things, more people listen. I personally owe these thinkers a great debt. I am trying to be one of the white males who is listening to what they have had to say and who believes them.

My students have heard and wrestled with what I have written here. They too have been a great resource for the development of these ideas, especially those students who have journelled their way through my "Religious Perspectives on Selfhood and Sexuality," the graduate students who argued with me in my seminars on "Religion and Gender," and students in other courses who have heard my guest lectures.

Fellow members of the Lawrence Men's Group have encouraged me and listened to portions of the evolving manuscript.

Many others have read portions of the material found here

and some all of it. They represent a variety of backgrounds, perspectives, and sexual orientations. They have encouraged me and given me much good advice, not all of which I have taken. The list includes, Paul Smith, Mel White, Urvashi Vaid, L. William Countryman, Marilyn Klaus, Paul and Shelly Haughey, Paul Bonin-Rodriguez, Will Sherwood, Tim Malone, Mahrya Monson, Robert Klein, Lindsey Gaston, Thad Holcomb, Mike Silverman, Richard Bryan, and David Commerford. So, I am fully responsible for what appears here and hoping to continue to learn more as I interact with people over these issues.

I want to thank Mahrya Monson and Brenda Bobo-Fisher of HumanityWorks! for their encouragement and support. They are far more than publishers. They are my loving, long-term friends of justice, compassion, and humanity. And finally I want to thank Gary Rockhold for designing the cover, laying out the text, and providing me with much more that has made the time in which I completed this project one of the best of my life.

This book is dedicated to all who have gone before me in the struggles for acceptance and affirmation of any people who have been discriminated against, demonized, hurt, killed, and marginalized because they did not fit the dominant idea of what it is to be human. It is dedicated to those who have given their lives, or had lives taken from them, because those human beings did not "fit in." It is dedicated to those whom our institutions shunned and condemned — some institutions even while believing this is compatible with "unconditional love" — because our culture needed scapegoats to blame for its failures. And it is dedicated to those who come after me who I believe will see that living in fears, such as being "scared straight," is no way for any human being to walk on our earth. Finally, it is dedicated to my circle of good friends who have loved and supported me through better or worse, sickness and health, love and loss, and everything in between. I look forward with excitement to the continual widening of that circle through this book and through meeting others who are on this journey out of fear, isolation, and the limits society imposes on us (the "straight" role) and toward the reappearance of their humanity. The world awaits the reemergence of such human, human beings again.

CHAPTER ONE

SOMETHING DEEPER IS GOING ON HERE

Newspaper articles, television images, and popular magazines feature emotionally charged groups arguing about gay people. Gay Pride marches are met with demonstrators who shout that transgendered and bisexual people and lesbians and gay men deserve discrimination and punishment. Radio talk show hosts declare gay people deviants, biological accidents, and even worthy of death.

Though the mainstream media focused on the death of Wyoming college student Matthew Shepherd, who was brutally beaten and left to die on a fence in 1999, one set of statistics says that one gay man is killed every two weeks in America just for being gay. Yet most gay bashings go unreported or ignored.

Anti-gay groups are formed with the single goal of stopping the progress of equal rights for gay people. Christian preachers and television evangelists shout from their physical and electronic pulpits about a "gay agenda" that is destroying America and its institutions. They proclaim that gay people deserve the eternal agony of hell.

"Ex-gay" groups work to "convert" women and men from something called a "gay lifestyle," while also admitting the difficulty, or even the impossibility, of ever leaving the orientation itself. The largest of these organizations, Exodus International, was founded by two "ex-gay" men who eventually became life partners and left the organization. Yet none of these groups can provide long term statistics to follow up on their efforts. Most admit they don't maintain such data, and some admit that their work is ineffective in changing anyone, though their clients can learn to act "straight."

Lesbian couples in rural United States who are just trying to live alone in peace are harassed by outsiders, even found brutally murdered. Communities where gay couples have been virtually ignored for years respond to national anti-gay agendas by demonizing and harassing their long-term neighbors.

Religious denominations are fractured just for discussing the affirmation of gay people. In the year 2000 the national conventions of the United Methodist Church, the Southern Baptists, the Presbyterians, and the Episcopal churches included demonstrations, sometimes even on the convention floors, which brought arrests of the demonstrators and statements from the floor which continued to affirm that gay people are less than those who are straight.

Politicians, such as Mississippi Senator Trent Lott on a radio talk show, compare gay people to alcoholics and kleptomaniacs. Parents cast out their children when they learn they are gay. When gay people ask for equality and equal rights, they are accused of asking for "special rights."

Just raising the possibility that gay, lesbian, bisexual or transgendered people should be tolerated or accepted like straight people increases the volume and temperature of discussion. Unfortunately, far more heat than light is shed on the subject. For example, what happens in the United States when a serviceman rumored to be gay looks too long at a fellow serviceman? The soldier is trained to be a fearless fighting machine. Yet the look can trigger a reaction so violent that he needs to destroy "the look" forever. One is beaten with a baseball bat while asleep in his bunk. Another's head is smashed repeatedly into a urinal until his face is unrecognizable. It's as if a look is a far greater personal threat than the gunfire of any foreign enemy. These "straight" soldiers report that they feel vulnerable, just as women do around men.

Few things still seem to disrupt our society today more than talking openly about understanding, defining, accepting, or even just tolerating people who identify as gay, lesbian, bisexual or transgendered. Though this is one among many human issues that involve discrimination and prejudice, even some of the immediate victims of the prejudices of race and class turn and run as far as possible in the opposite direction when faced with the issue of equal rights for "those people." Distance from this issue feels like safety. Many victimized people seem especially relieved to be able to say, "*At least* I'm not gay. And don't ever compare their discrimination to mine."

We hear objections that invoke every institution of our society to stifle the mere attempt to discuss the possibility that gay, lesbian, bisexual and transgendered people should be treated equally. Sometimes, we're told, it is against the "family," sometimes against the children, sometimes against "Motherhood," sometimes against God, sometimes against the so-called "Judeo-Christian" tradition, sometimes it is against a "healthy" life-style, sometimes against "the American Way." We hear arguments that are religious, social, economic, and political. Beliefs rooted in assumptions about the nature of the family or the nature of Nature, and so on, stifle any consideration of the mere possibility of equality, value, and normalcy for gay people.

People who prefer to frame any such discussion only in negative terms hunt for arguments and precedents from every source. Those who want a more objective discussion are often drowned out by the volume, the cute sound bites, and the relentless, continual, and multiple strategies of vehement opponents. As a result, even the defenders of gay people respond with just as much emotion and often with hardly more insight into what is happening.

SOME THINGS THAT DON'T MAKE SENSE

However, some things about all of this turmoil just don't add up. We only need to look at a couple of curious but common events in our society. Begin with that entrenched American cultural icon: the Bible. In the book of the prophet Ezekiel found in the Hebrew Scriptures, which Christians call the "Old Testament," we read in chapter 16 and verse 49 a description of the infamous city of Sodom and its sins: "Now this was the sin of your sister Sodom: She and her daughters were arrogant, overfed and unconcerned; they did not help the poor and the needy." Now this is a very clear statement from the same Bible in which we find the story of the twin cities of Sodom and Gomorrah (Genesis 19), a statement which explains how the writers of the Bible understood the real sin of their inhabitants. The city of Sodom (and its Sodomites?) was an infamous example in early history of a society that cared nothing for those among it who were the most in need, "the poor and the needy."

Curiously, this early and biblical reputation of the city is not the one that has been passed down to us in popular culture. Instead, one of the oddities of Western culture is the fact that "sodomy" has been defined as something else, not what the biblical writers themselves clearly said it was. Even today, in spite of the overwhelming historical and literary evidence, many people remain convinced that this other popular interpretation is exactly what the ancient story of Sodom and Gomorrah meant back then and means even now for twenty-first century society.

If the Bible itself tells us that "sodomy" is the sin of lack of concern for the needy, the question becomes: why is "sodomy" defined in terms of sex in our culture? Why are many Christian ministers who boldly proclaim they speak for God and the Bible, so adamant about using the word "sodomy" and referring to "the sin of Sodom and Gomorrah," to talk about sex, particularly homosexual sex? Why do our "sodomy" laws and our politicians and courts do the same thing? And why is the above passage from Ezekiel and numerous other fairly obvious biblical verses in both the Old and New Testaments ignored by, or unconvincing to, so many people? The popular understanding clings desperately to the sexualized and anti-gay interpretation which this generation, in turn, has heard from those before it. We have even come to call this "the traditional" understanding, even though it is neither the earliest interpretation nor the only one known today.

Another curious reaction still common in the United States at the beginning of the twenty-first century is that if any self-identified heterosexual woman refuses to follow society's ideas of female beauty (which have been defined mostly by males), refuses to find her worth in male approval, refuses to find all her needs fulfilled by men, does not marry at an early enough age, and stands publicly with her sisters against any kind of discrimination against women, she will probably be suspected of being, and ridiculed and joked about as, a lesbian.

Remember the jokes that circulated around former first lady, Hillary Clinton? They hit their peak early in her husband's presidency when she volunteered to be the public spokesperson for healthcare reform. She appeared to be a strong, self-assured, and focused woman. She also appeared to be liberated from male judgments. She was even suspected of doing what only men are supposed to do: acting in her own best interests as she herself defined them. Even though she was married and would "stand by her man" through relentless criticism, popular humor questioned her sexuality. This curious example illustrates the fact that the label "lesbian" will be applied to women when the issue at hand has little to do with who is in love with whom or who is literally "in bed" with whom.

Then there is another interesting reaction common to our culture. If any two self-identified heterosexual men were to walk down almost any street in America and hold hands or put their arms around each other — as male friends do in many other countries of the world — they will be treated the way gay men are treated and even "gay-bashed." Does violence against gay men have anything to do with sex or love, or is the real issue something else we need to examine?

Some deeper, extremely important dynamic which this book seeks to explore is going on below the surface in all these cases. It is "something" quite basic that touches how we in our society define ourselves and affirm who we are. This dynamic is something that people act out on anyone who appears to be different from some broadly acceptable, societal definitions of who we are. We take it out on anyone who is, or appears to be, gay, lesbian, bisexual, or transgendered. This "something" touches our society much deeper than all of the usual reasons given for criticizing, stereotyping, condemning, and bashing gay people. Gay people appear to be the scapegoats for whatever this is.

The reactions we observe are intense, entrenched, highly emotional, often irrational, and disproportionate to any real personal threats. Gay men, for example, are not just killed but run over repeatedly, cut into pieces, beaten beyond recognition, or slowly tortured to death. The intensity of the responses indicates that these reactions arise out of more than mere misunderstandings or gaps in the information we possess. Something in our gut keeps us chained to misinformation and produces rage, hate, anger, fear, and obsession.

These reactions produce far more hate crimes than are ever reported. They surface in violent words and actions, in threats of everlasting and even worse violence in the next world for souls who disagree, in claims that many of our fellow human beings are not human, and in rhetorical pronouncements that our very civilization is threatened by homosexuality. They appear in the passionate rejection of children whom parents previously swore they loved, in the demise of friendships, in the firing of competent people in our workplaces, and in the witch hunts of the military and other traditionally "masculine" organizations.

All sorts of actions and feelings that most of us would judge to be highly irrational in other contexts arise out of this deep-seated dynamic. We might suspect that these reactions rise out of some terror deep within us. There is a reason for all of this turmoil, but the reasons we usually get from our mainstream sources of information don't seem to explain the depth and intensity of these reactions.

Psychologists have taught us that such deep-seated emotions and the violent actions that often follow must be traceable to conditions in our early childhood. Something happens to us very early in life that lays the foundation for these strange responses. Something instills in us the deep-seated feeling that the acceptance of gay people will upset some crucial societal and personal equilibrium. Accepting them, we sincerely feel, will destroy society like a sin or a cancer similar to the reputed "immorality" that destroyed the Roman Empire. And behind this may actually be the fear that such acceptance will demand major changes in our very familiar and prized definitions of who we are.

Many historians and students of other cultures have been struck by the fact that most of the key definitions of ourselves and others which we cling to are peculiar to the twentieth-century, and especially to the United States or Northern Europe. Anthropologist Stuart Schlegel is one who writes passionately about the alternative to these understandings he found among the Teduray, a rainforest people on the Philippine island of Mindanao. Many of our most cherished, core beliefs about humanity, violence, sexuality, manhood, femininity, and sexual orientation, were challenged as he lived among these tolerant, gentle, noncompetitive people. Their ideals contrasted sharply with those that we have been taught are essential to humanity.

The Teduray could not grasp our acceptance of the necessity of violence. They did not accept that our labels of "homosexuality" and "heterosexuality" were ways to understand, much less judge, human beings. They never thought of the sexual act as we did. And they couldn't accept our beliefs that there are distinctly different roles for men and women. In other words, much of what our culture teaches is natural to humans they thought was strangely unnatural.

Yet our educational experiences have taught us to believe that these ideas which people like the Teduray reject are not really bound to our particular time and place, or to our particular cultural circumstances. Instead, we sincerely believe they are universal and absolute definitions of who we and others are. We really feel that they are "natural" and even that they are God-given. So, we read them back into our ancient texts and our authoritative traditions even if they were not there to begin with.

The Authorities We Use for Cover

In some ways it comforts us to "find" our favorite and familiar beliefs, feelings, and definitions in traditions and texts, religious and otherwise, that we believe are authoritative. We might appeal to the religious or non-religious traditions we use to define us and maintain our distinct identity when we feel threatened. We might appeal to the leaders of institutions on which we rely for stability and truth. In the United States, dominated as it is by Protestant Christianity, the Bible is one of the most commonly used cultural examples of such "authority."

We might further believe that our ideas, feelings, and beliefs, actually originated in these authorities. We might have convinced ourselves that they are not merely our culture's

ideas or merely our interpretations of ancient texts and traditions or only one of the many possible ways of understanding
things. We come to believe that these ideas and feelings are
universal, not just the result of our twentieth-century,
American experiences. And believing this can be comforting to
most of us. If these ideas and feelings are not just our own
ideas and opinions, then we aren't required to shoulder the
personal responsibility for the definitions, ideas, and understandings. Their validity depends on the "authorities."

So instead of believing that our understanding of these
"authorities" is merely an interpretation which came from our
own learned prejudices and the prejudices of the cultural interpreters whom we choose to follow, we believe that our understanding is what the traditions and texts *really* say. As a result,
we need not feel responsible for the ideas and prejudices we
hold. The texts and traditions, and even God, are responsible.
We don't have to be on the line and alone with these ideas.
They are not our ideas but the Truth itself. "I wouldn't hate gay
people, or consider being gay a sin," we can say, "but God
does, so I have to." In this way we portray ourselves as nice
people. God is the real rat.

If instead we were to begin with, "The way I understand this
is," or "I believe," or "My interpretation of this verse is," we
would put the whole responsibility in our own lap. It would
mean we ourselves would have to question the people who
told us that these are *the* meanings. It would mean we ourselves are the ones who must examine and evaluate alternative
interpretations and alternative understandings. We might even
have to re-evaluate our current ideas. We would have to take
responsibility for our beliefs about ourselves and about those
"others" who in some ways may not be like the mainstream.

It's much easier just to accept what the authorities, the traditions, the preachers, and the teachers say. Then we are not
alone with these ideas and we won't have to feel personally
vulnerable for holding them. We are surrounded by the securi-

ty of their company. So, with Pontius Pilate, the infamous Roman governor who sent Jesus to his death, we can "wash our hands" of the responsibility for these ideas and beliefs. We won't have to do any of the hard, self-examining, personal work that may threaten to overthrow our current definitions and judgments, and maybe even our prejudices and our comfortable communities.

But the Bible Says...

How people use the Bible regarding the issue of gay, lesbian, bisexual, and transgendered people provides an illuminating example of this use of such "authorities." The popular argument uses seven Biblical passages which are believed to be against either homosexuality or homosexual activities. Those who argue this way declare: "The Bible says," or "God says," not "As I understand the Bible," or "I interpret the Bible to say." The responsibility for their views is placed on the Bible or God, not on their understanding of the texts. Others, accepting these arguments and interpretations as actually "what the Bible says," but who want to support gay, lesbian, bisexual, or transgendered people, have understandably either given up on the Bible or responded, "I don't take it literally."

This assumes, of course, that the popular interpretation is a literal interpretation of what these texts intend to say. The popular interpreters will tell us this: "It's the plain sense of scripture." But no one interprets the whole Bible literally. Without exception, every interpreter takes some passages literally and some allegorically, poetically, symbolically, and/or culturally — anything but literally. Phrases like "God makes the clouds His chariot," "let the hills sing for joy," or "let the floods clap their hands," are never considered literal descriptions of God's means of movement, the communication methods of hills, or the anatomy of flood waters. No wonder there are about 3,000 Christian denominations in America today which claim to be based on what the Bible really says, but still can't agree on what that is.

In addition, these self-identified "literalists" declare that some passages are no longer relevant to our current culture. They offer numerous theories of Biblical interpretation to distinguish which passages apply to us now and which passages do not.

One of the most popular is the historically unsupportable interpretation that some laws in the Hebrew Bible are moral laws, others civil laws, and still others ceremonial laws. The "Ten Commandments" are often considered central to the moral law, but seldom quoted, much less posted, in their full Biblical versions which show what they meant in early Hebrew culture when women were not to be "coveted" along with the other property of their male owners. Laws restricting activities on the "Sabbath" (literally the "seventh" day of the week) most often in America interpreted as Sunday (the first day of the week), were once enforced widely through "Blue Laws," state laws restricting business on those days. Now they are interpreted by most as ceremonial at best. Thus they are now dispensable. For these interpreters, only what they now interpret to be the moral laws are relevant today.

Of course, this distinction between kinds of biblical laws is not made explicitly in any biblical passage, whether it is in the Old or New Testaments. It was never made by traditional Judaism. Yet it functions popularly for numerous Bible users to enable them to justify why they can ignore certain commandments while they enforce the ones which support their current understandings of the way things should be.

Another popular, modern, western notion of biblical interpretation holds that certain biblical passages are meant for the age we live in (often called "this dispensation") while others are only for previous or future ages. These interpreters divide history into different periods so that some verses, and even whole books, of the Bible can just be ignored today. So, though the Hebrew book of Leviticus condemns the touching of a pigskin, a well-known contemporary preacher and football star, does not believe that this Leviticus passage is relevant to him. He has made a name for himself, however, by regularly using another Leviticus verse, "Thou shall not lie with mankind as with womankind, for it is an abomination." That one, he asserts, is an eternal law of God. He is far from alone in his selectivity.

"Literalists" use the Bible selectively to support the current, dominant opinions regarding these deeply entrenched issues. In addition, when these selected passages are acceptable to the literalists' theories of interpretation, they consider their own interpretation not merely one of the possible interpretations but *the* Truth, *the* word of God. Contemporary Biblical scholars offer a number of interpretations of each of the seven Biblical passages which are used regarding homosexuality, and have written much about them. Since only one of these ways of interpreting the seven passages is negative toward homosexual acts, the question is why that one is popular. The answer is, because it supports the current, dominant cultural understanding of the issue.

In addition, people who use the Bible choose to ignore, or not take literally, passages that do not support their culture's dominant teachings. Few American Christians believe that Jesus' call to a rich man to "Give all you have to the poor and follow me," is personally relevant to them in twenty-first century, affluent, consumer-oriented America. Few recommend that we take literally Jesus' teaching: "It is easier for a camel to go through the eye of a needle than for a rich man to enter the kingdom of heaven." The suggested alternatives some propose to the idea that the word "needle" means a literal needle are humorous, if not desperate.

Who in our capitalist country will preach about the literal meaning of the Old Testament law against collecting interest on loans, even though the biblical prophets repeated that law more than most others? In a culture where most of our money is made through interest on loans and investments and where we now culturally define "usury" as not charging "too much" interest (in some cases the limit is not over 300% APR), we won't take this literally. We can't, because if we ever were to do so, we would have to admit that our whole economic system is against the Bible, and even anti-God.

More to the point of this book, five times in the New Testament the early Christians were told to "greet" each other with a kiss. In one case the apostle Paul told his protege, a fellow, male minister named Timothy: "Greet all the brothers with a holy kiss." This may be the second most repeated command in the entire New Testament, if we put all the commands to love one another together as the first.

Does this mean that men kissing men or even men kissing women is the normal greeting in American churches? Of course not. And the reason why those who take the seven passages they use against gay people as eternal, absolute truth but dismiss this simple and clear command is because, they say, this command is culturally relative. It should not, they believe, be applied "literally." One paraphrase out of England translated the command to Timothy as "Greet all the brothers with a hearty handshake!" The obvious question would be, if this command is culturally relative, why not the other verses that are used in this discussion? The answer is that the Bible is being used to uphold current cultural values, here a homophobic one.

This, of course, is far from the first time the Bible has been used to support the elements of a dominant cultural agenda. History overflows with examples. The Bible was used to support crusades and other religious wars, the belief that the deaf were unable to hear the Gospel, the theory that the earth was the center of the galaxy, the belief that women should never teach men, the burning of hundreds of thousands as witches, the dogma that the only purpose of sexual activity even in marriage is procreation, the Inquisition, the destruction of one "Christian" group by another throughout Europe and America, as well as antisemitism, racism, and other prejudices. Colonial America was rife with persecutions of all sorts which were supported by people quoting the Bible — the Baptists, the Catholics, and the Quakers, to name only a few who were victims. All these persecutions were sanctioned with quotations from biblical passages.

The Ku Klux Klan still quotes the Bible in its antisemitic, anti-Catholic, white supremacist and anti-gay rhetoric. Passages from the Hebrew Bible which no academic scholar would identify as references to "the White race," such as Deuteronomy 7:6 and I Kings 11:2, are seriously interpreted as commands to Northern European and American Protestants to separate themselves from all other peoples, including the Hebrews to whom the passages clearly are addressed. Such a use of the Bible would be humorous, if it weren't so tragic, destructive, and fatal.

For nineteen hundred years, the dominant Christian interpretation of the Bible supported slavery. Most Western pulpits rang with the conviction that this is: "What the Bible says."

Frankly, if we take the verses in the Bible which explicitly mention slavery and slaves literally, it is difficult to find support for an abolitionist position. Slavery is always used as a positive paradigm for Christians. Slaves are regularly told, particularly in the New Testament, that they are to obey their masters as they would God even if their masters treated them cruelly. There is no literal command to end slavery.

On top of this, numerous passages which have nothing to do with the enslavement of people of color, were also interpreted to support slavery. One example, the famous "Curse of Ham" in Genesis 9:25, still turns up in attempts to preach that Black people were cursed by God so they are born to serve the other races! In its Genesis context, it was Ham's son, Canaan, who was cursed in order to provide justification for the destruction of the Canaanites by the Israelites when they entered Palestine. But this did not prevent the popular

American use of Genesis 9:25 to justify the oppression of people of color.

Something, however, happened to question the dominant, traditional, "literal" understanding of the Bible's view of slavery. It was not the discovery of new Bible manuscripts. It was not that new pages or books were added to the Bible. In fact, the change took place over the curses and violent condemnations of traditional believers who were certain that their interpretations were the literal word of God. America's largest Protestant denomination, the Southern Baptist Convention was founded in 1845 to maintain slavery as a system sanctioned by God in the Bible. After all, we must admit, those pro-slavery Bible believers had a long tradition to support their interpretation. There is no question that the pro-slavery understanding was "the traditional" one. And that is an effective argument only if "tradition" is presumed authoritative.

What began to change were cultural attitudes toward slavery and, in a few cases, its accompanying prejudices. As these new attitudes became more and more pervasive, they could no longer be marginalized and ignored by the larger culture. Eventually, when these cultural attitudes became the dominant ones, people's interpretations of the Bible changed.

It is difficult to imagine how revolutionary this change of interpretation was because this new understanding is now both entrenched and representative of our cultural norms. This very discussion of the Bible's past use to support slavery and of how recent in world history this radical change of interpretation came about, seems quaint, archaic, and even offensive to people who don't want to admit that the Bible can be, and, therefore, may still be, used this horribly when judged by today's non-traditional standards. It is strategically important for many who use the Bible to distance themselves from such historical evidence in order to protect the "truth" of their current interpretations. That was then, they feel, but this is now when we know better what God says.

THIS IS ABOUT US, NOT AUTHORITIES

What people claim the Bible and the authority of traditions say, therefore, is a good measure of cultural attitudes and prejudices. The popular interpretations are the ones that support the culture's prejudices. Even a cursory glance through history indicates that what the Bible itself or authoritative traditions really say or mean is apparently not the basic issue behind such attitudes. Yet people use the Bible and "tradition" as if they were the keys to cultural attitudes.

The power of arguments from the Bible and tradition is great, however. That power is not found in the fact that the Bible and tradition are the origins of these ideas, but in the power of the societal positions they justify which are deep-seated in our culture and its institutions, in our feelings, and in our minds.

To argue about the Bible with people, then, is to skirt the real, personal and societal issues and never get to that "something" that is lying behind these interpretations. This is true even though those who argue for their prejudices really believe that it is the Bible that propels their beliefs. What they have been taught in institutions that have provided them with more than mere intellectual teaching, but with personal meaning, comfort, acceptance, a community, and social standing, while threatening them with guilt, discipline, and unending punishment, is hard for the committed to re-think and re-feel. It's hard because we are dealing with "something" deeper even than arguments over the Bible and tradition, something taught to us early in life through non-rational means.

When it comes to texts and traditions which people in the past and present have used to justify even opposing positions, we can only take full responsibility for our own positions in these matters. "I believe," "I think," "No, I believe this is right," must be repeated until people are ready to look beneath these texts and traditions in order to do some difficult and personal work.

Once the real issues emerge from under the Biblical and traditional covers, we need to dig down to core cultural beliefs, definitions, images, and feelings that we hold inside us. These indicate what is really going on here.

To find out what this deeper dynamic at the core of the issue of accepting transgendered and bisexual people and lesbians and gay men is, it will help us to trace the nature of the process of learning our cultural definitions along with the emotions that accompany these definitions. We need to examine the mechanisms which teach and enforce the ideas and definitions we cherish. Their stubborn hold on us, the feeling that they are immutably true, and the means by which we learned them, keep most of us from questioning these definitions of who we are. It is difficult to challenge them even if by clinging to these definitions, images, and ideas we are kept from living fully as human beings.

FURTHER READING

Daniel A. Helminiak, *What the Bible Really Says About Homosexuality.* 2nd ed. San Francisco: Alamo Square Press, 2000.

Mark D. Jordon, *The Invention of Sodomy in Christian Theology.* Chicago: University of Chicago Press, 1997.

Stuart A. Schlegel, *Wisdom from a Rainforest: The Spiritual Journey of an Anthropologist.* Athens: University of Georgia Press, 1999.

CHAPTER TWO

HOW DID IT GET SO DEEP INSIDE?

The eye surgeon said I needed an operation to correct the torn and detached retina in my right eye. I had been fortunate that this would be the first operation I would experience in my life. I had always taken my health for granted and thought that operations happened only to other people. But when he told me that I was going progressively blind and the alternative was complete blindness, I was jolted into the realization, not just the idea, that I was vulnerable. Even with all my interest in taking care of myself, I now knew experientially that there was a fragility about my life. That personal experience literally and figuratively helped me see things differently.

We seldom see the real issues that underlie the ills of our life and society until we are jolted out of our everyday existence by some traumatic or otherwise unforgettable experience. It seems that to "wake up" to what is really going on behind the normal, acceptable lives we are making for ourselves according to society's formula for success and happiness, we often need to experience considerable discomfort with "the way things are" and with how they are being explained and justified.

The ancient tale of the Buddha (whose name means "one who has awakened") provides an example of a person who was jolted into such an "awakening." This 6th century B.C.E. Indian prince left a legendary affluent lifestyle, one which his society assured him was "fulfilling" and "secure." He wandered from teacher to teacher but was dissatisfied with all their explanations of reality. In desperation he sat down alone. After long meditation and internal struggles, the most basic truths broke through the sleep of his everyday life and he "awoke." The real issues hit him.

Even though the Buddha's followers give the label "enlightenment" to the insight he received while he sat in meditation, he also "awoke" earlier. An important, previous set of events first provoked him to question his accepted view of reality and wonder if there were an alternative. It convinced him to leave the comfortable position he had inherited in order to strike out in search of answers to new questions which were making him uncomfortable in the middle of his comfort. Without that initial awakening and the questions it raised, he would have remained stuck in the view of reality he had inherited, dreaming and hardly ever knowing he was asleep.

WE ARE WET AND DON'T KNOW IT

Like the pre-enlightened Indian prince, we too live on the basis of the definitions and ideas about reality our culture gives us. And we do so without much reflection about them. Who has the time and the financial resources to stop everything else and sit and question this dominant view of reality we inherited? Who has the energy to ask larger questions after a long day at the office, the store, or the factory, followed by the demands of our families and our need to maintain a lifestyle that we too have been taught is "fulfilling"?

When we do seek information and understanding about our culture, we receive very little. The media opt more and more for sound bites, short news briefs which reduce everything to the "World News in One Minute," or personal interest angles which oversimplify and divert us from complicated stories about the direction of our society. These bites, briefs, and angles substitute for stories that dig into the issues that might otherwise challenge our sleepy world or shake the stability of corporate media owners and their sponsors.

Television has become our major source of information, but studies by university communication departments have shown that the more we rely on it for news, the less we understand the issues. The triumph of the "USA Today" style newspaper, with its emphasis on sports, color pictures, short stories, and lightly treated features, is evidence that the news we get is "Newsac," like the elevator music that lulls us into the mainstream mood without any challenging and discordant chords to shake our sensibilities.

What hinders us not only from carefully examining "hot button" issues like the variety of human sexual orientations, but also from even bringing them up at all, is the fact that we are awash in the conditioning of our culture. We are like fish in water. The water unremittingly surrounds the fish without calling attention to itself. They never live in an alternative to the wetness against their scales. They know nothing but water and live in terms of its nourishment and support. We too are, in reality, "wet."

We also have no experience, recollection, or consciousness of experiencing any alternatives to being immersed in the "water" that surrounds us. So, even if we are able to wrap our minds around the idea that there could be alternatives, we not only don't see what they are, but we aren't even sure they exist or that they are possible alternatives. First, someone or some event needs to convince us that we are "wet." Then, since the water has become comfortable and familiar, we have to be willing to face the insecurity of knowing that "wet" isn't the only way things have to be.

Even though there are outward differences among fish which provide some variety within the common wetness, and though fish might even disagree about how best to swim in the water around them, they all share the water. In the same way, our "wetness" is the basic, deep-rooted, view of reality in which we are immersed. It is pervasive and all-encompassing because it is reinforced everywhere in our society. All of our institutions are wrapped up in the ideas, images, emotions, and judgments that make up the view of reality that we have come to feel is natural, universal, and eternally fixed. We cannot believe this way of seeing things is only culturally constructed and temporal. Our institutions support, teach, base their own success upon, interrelate in terms of, maintain, and enforce this view. Few people successfully stand outside it. Unless we remember our pre-effected life in very early childhood, we have few resources and references in the present which we can use to examine the culture's "wetness."

This is understandable. We were all thrown in the water early. Throughout our life this view of reality — which consists of goals, ideas, images, myths, symbols, feelings, and values — was systematically instilled in us. For example, we were taught to take the following ideas for granted as self-evident and to begin with these ideas when we relate to everything and everyone about us:

- Democracy is the best and the most evolved form of government.

- Competition is good for people. It produces cheaper and better things as well as better people, and that is good for everyone.

- Progress is good and it should not be stopped. This takes the form of what we call "development" of the earth, of our people, and of our resources. "Underdeveloped" countries are those behind in such progress.

- Newer is better than older. We ask, "Is this the latest book or opinion on that subject" as if the latest is better than the oldest.

- Youth is preferred to old age. Younger is closer to beauty.

- What's good for "the economy" (usually meaning big business) is good for people.

- The economy should always be growing at a "healthy" rate.

- Free market forces will produce what is right and moral.

- The family of origin should be preserved, even at great cost to the psychological and physical health of its members.

These are some basic ideas that make up the dominant way of seeing reality in our culture, though they are not the ones we will be looking at in this book. Whether they are true or not, and even though they have not been universally accepted, they have been ingrained in us so that we begin our thinking with these assumptions and usually argue over how best to implement them.

It's the Software for Our Operating System

Some institutions taught our basic way to see and understand reality directly while others supported it either implicitly or through the consent of their silence. Even these silent ones assumed its truth.

The values we embraced and the rules of this game of life we were expected to follow without question, were installed in us somewhat like the installation of software in a computer. We were never asked whether these were the rules we wanted to play by. Instead, people who "knew better" than we did, the experts, the adults around us, were expected to successfully install these values and ideas in us. We were trained to live by them alone.

If the process of installation was successful, we were made to feel that nothing anywhere would run without this system. The alternatives we could envision were chaos, destruction, disease, and death. We may feel that like fish we will die without the water. And, most likely, the system's view of reality became our own operating system before we had the freedom to ask if this were really the system we wanted to live by. And we were off, growing up with these rules, and their accompanying definitions as "Truth." Our own success in the variety of institutions about us as children, such as our families and our schools, depended upon us running our lives by these "Truths."

We were raised in families which were governed by adults who in turn were brought up with the elements of this view of reality coming at them from everywhere. Acceptance of this dominant view, at least outwardly, was usually necessary for the financial and social success of these adults. Passing this view of reality along to their children also defined their "success" at being what they were told were "good" parents.

It didn't matter whether parents used what psychologist Alice Miller argues is the "poisonous pedagogy" which makes up the child-rearing methods of our culture and subordinates the child's humanity to parental needs. This pedagogy believes the infant and small child are innately selfish and abusive to others and therefore in need of being trained, at times even in physically and emotionally abusive ways, to be unselfish and caring. Our parents, and theirs before them, sincerely believed that what they taught us about reality was, as one of Miller's books is entitled, "For Your Own Good." Some parents may have questioned pieces of the dominant view of reality they were taught, or even rebelled against them, but these were the exceptions. Most were afraid that their children would not "succeed" in a system they knew could be cruel to "failures."

We soon began moving outside our parents' realm of full control, though a number of parents further fought this move, feeling threatened by their loss of control. They attempted to limit our outside experiences and schooling to "wholesome" ones through private and parochial institutions that more closely reinforced their teachings.

Yet, even if they seemed to fail to keep us within their limits, it was really only a failure to teach us to swim in the water the same way they did. We actually moved into an educational system that at its deepest level assumed and promoted their root teachings, for the primary purpose of schools was to mold us into "good citizens." This was hardly different from the basic parental view of reality because the policy makers on the local school boards represented "us," the people within the structures whose success also depended upon conforming to the dominant cultural values.

WE ARE EDUCATED APPROPRIATELY

Making people "good citizens" meant, first and foremost, that we were taught the "approved" and "acceptable" curriculum through "approved" and "acceptable" means. "Approved" and "acceptable" were the key words because that curriculum could not threaten the official operating system. It had to teach us to approve of what is and to make what is "better" at what it essentially is. The agenda included teaching what society decided were the "appropriate" and societally affirming choices of historical materials, people, events, ideas, and interpretations to study. We learned the myths of our culture, the stories, true or not, which installed the view of reality. We may have learned, for example, that George Washington, "the father of our country," never told a lie. Anyone who said he may have been more human than that was un-American.

Our schools also installed an "appropriate" reverence for certain social and governmental structures as well as the "appropriate" means for examining them. We were taught to vote Democrat or Republican, to get a nine-to-five job, to worship big business and its needs, to vilify Communism and "welfare states," to believe that the United States is always the best, and on and on. We learned that it was "inappropriate" to ask questions that were too "radical." Even in the area where our schools were supposed to value creativity, they taught "appreciation" of "appropriate" (or "good") art and music.

We were taught how to learn and were expected to do so "on schedule" or we would fail. Though we were born natural learners who from the very first used every means we had to learn about our world — our mouths being the most sensitive instrument of exploration, we had to change our methods. Our inborn process of learning would be too chaotic and too individually centered to mesh with society's purposes for us. As New York State Teacher of the Year for 1991, John Taylor Gatto, describes it, schools were teaching something more basic than the subjects we were expected to master, such as mathematics, English, and foreign languages. They were teaching ideas and attitudes about ourselves and how we must learn. Award-winning teachers teach "school," he points out, not children. They make students conform and fit in rather than challenge the structures that stifle them.

This meant that for twelve more years of our life, we were taught not only to accept the dominant institutional structures around us but also to accept that view of reality they embodied as inherently, even universally, good. Both our formal and informal education taught us that the blame for problems, or any lack of "success" within these institutions, should be placed squarely on the shoulders of deviant individuals. Those who don't "make it," we were taught, must be lazy, inept, ungifted, untalented, of bad ancestry, or rebellious. This further reinforced the parental teaching that children are inferior to adults in knowledge, moral understanding, and civility, and that parent-child problems are the child's fault and responsibility. If society did blame parents for their children's problems, it faulted parents for not teaching the system and our place in it well enough.

It was not "appropriate, affirming, helpful," even "American," to imply that the problem is in the culture of the dominant institutions themselves. Sometimes the ultimate reason given for human failures was explained by the direct teaching of some inherent human sinfulness. At other times this was said less directly with casual references to the inherent problems with "human nature" to explain what appear to be common examples where humans and our institutions do not mesh. The repetition of the stories of American clergyman and juvenile fiction author Horatio Alger as if they were cultural myths, reinforced the teaching that an individual's self-reliance and hard work were all that was needed to achieve "success." Failures and deviations were our own fault. Challenging the health of the system itself, we soon learned, was clearly out of the question. It was a clear sign of "deviance."

For those twelve years our educational institutions taught us to be in awe of "the powers that be" within governmental, business, religious, educational, and other dominant institutions. The schools that won awards were the ones that were most "successful" by these standards. They received awards for instilling this awe the best and the most cost-effectively. We so internalized our indebtedness to these powers for our future financial and social security that we soon kept ourselves from questioning their teachings.

In contrast to what American historians like Howard Zinn in his *A People's History of the United States* have demonstrated, we were also taught that only through these powers could real "improvement" take place. Thus, our cultural heroes became presidents, congressional leaders, and masters of business, sports, entertainment, and media.

Unlike the rest of us, these leaders, we were told, do have "the right stuff," are born at "the right time," or are "natural" leaders. We might be able to be like them if we are both lucky and gifted. Even if most who try will fall short of those "role models," we learned that we should try anyway. It is, we were told, the trying that is important. We did not see that the effort and the growing stakes we sunk into the effort would actually keep us from questioning the whole game even if we felt we were not getting ahead or were falling behind. The greater the amount of our energies, money, and time we devoted to the chase, the harder it would be to take it all back, see it as a waste, and admit that, "Even if you win the rat race, you're still a rat."

We also learned that only a select and limited set of deviations from the rules, norms, roles, and cultural patterns that make up this way of seeing things, are acceptable. "You must learn the rules (of reasoning, grammar, economics, art, music, morality, etc) before you try to break them," we were told. This limited the scope of our creativity to rule-breaking, thereby keeping us in the value system. We came to know better than to ever again ask really creative, but what our culture devalued as "childish," questions, such as: "What if there were a fourth primary color?" No deviations should ever be great enough to challenge our structures and their deepest values.

It is surprising but heartening, that anyone who makes it through this constant barrage ever questions authority and effects deep change. People do, and they produce "unacceptable, questionable, inappropriate" art, music, theories, dreams, and movements. They disrupt and disturb the status quo. They confuse our view of reality like Galileo did in the 16th century when he was condemned by the Church for attempting to prove that the earth was not the center of the universe. It took four hundred years for the dominant institution to admit that its view was wrong and to declare him correct and no longer a heretic. People who question the cherished systematic assumptions like Galileo dared to do are often declared "disorderly" in conduct and "subversive" in their teachings.

There are more people who question and reject elements of the dominant view than our educational system and our corporate and religious media let us know. But to point these people out in their real numbers would threaten the structures. It would open us to what we would come to feel is a personal threat of radically alternative possibilities. Even when those who challenge the basic view of reality make it into mainstream histories, they are "cleaned up" before their stories are passed down to us. So, these histories fail to portray Helen Keller as the social activist she was, and they proclaim Martin Luther King Jr. as an activist against personal prejudices, but not as someone who questioned the American political and economic system that perpetuates them.

WE LEARN REAL CHANGE IS JUST NOT POSSIBLE

Instead, the most successful result of the culture's teaching was to instill a deep hopelessness in us about attempts for any foundational changes and a mistrust in those who dare to change things. In spite of all the "positive" messages about "achievement" schools, parents, and even the media gave us, we were also taught the impossibility of effecting any major changes. "There is no hope to make real change." "You can't fight city hall." "That's the way it's always been." "That's just the way things are." "This is the best it can be." Paul Rogat Loeb in *The Soul of a Citizen* identifies this hopelessness with the beliefs that our individual involvement is not worthwhile and that anything we might attempt to do to change things in the public sphere would be done in vain.

We are so filled with this core hopelessness that anyone who expresses hope seems out of touch with our more "realistic" view of it all. So we roll our eyes at and make jokes about the hopeful ones. We dismiss them as "dreamers," "childish," "not down to earth," "unrealistic" "do-gooders" and "way out there." If they are the focus of mainstream media, they are portrayed in a cartoonish fashion, as quirky, eccentric, weird, pathetic, and marginal characters whom we must tolerate.

Since our religious institutions, which are supposed to

instill faith, hope and love, are also a part of this system, their voices join in this dismissal of the possibility of real change. Instead, many justify and bless the current structure. Whether labeled "liberal" or "conservative," they teach theologies that sanctify the system. They teach a religious position that theologian H. Richard Niebuhr labeled "the Christ of Culture." God is used to baptize and support the structure as if it fell directly from heaven. In addition, many of these and other religious institutions substitute a hope that is beyond the grave or, at least, in a future so distant and divine (not at all like this human one) that we are saved from expecting the success of our attempts to really change things in this present age.

WE GET THE SAME MESSAGE FROM OUR "LIBERAL" COLLEGES

Our colleges and universities continued this conditioning beyond high school. Some professors, particularly in the humanities and social sciences, might have been liberal, progressive, or even radical enough when compared with the teachers of our first eighteen years, so that we responded or reacted to their alternative views of our culture. It felt as if these were the first teachers in our entire educational experience to push a "political agenda." Because their analyses of our culture and its institutions were so different from that of the view of reality we had been taught, their views stood out, and we may have bristled at them.

In our earlier years we did not notice that we were always being taught a political, social, and moral agenda because it was in sync with the dominant view we received from everywhere. But these professors intellectually and emotionally challenged the comfortable view of reality we had already internalized. Taken seriously, they might have made us question the system. Did we need a new operating system? Was there a Macintosh that would work just as well as, or even better than, our DOS?

The more conservative critics of our institutions of higher

education responded by labeling them "liberal" or "radical" and, earlier, "Communist" or "Socialist." They attacked the concept of tenure for faculty, under the unsubstantiated guise that tenure actually makes professors, who are notorious workaholics, lazy. The real issue was that the loss of tenure would guarantee that no professors will deviate beyond the view of reality that is "acceptable." At last there will be no "acceptable" institutions to worry about where anyone can challenge the existing structures without suffering financial penalties.

In reality, as institutions, our colleges and universities are far from liberal. Though some individual professors may be "radical," universities as societal institutions seldom effectively challenge the basic structure. Their value is more often defined in terms of how they uphold the things. As public financing decreases and grant-getting from private sources with corporate ties is rewarded, they become further wed to the success of the system. Drug research is funded by the companies who will profit from positive results. Oil companies underwrite much of the geological research. Food manufacturers are funding many of our nutritional studies.

Most colleges and universities have departments or even schools of business, whose purpose is to further the goals of big business. How many have schools of labor? In business schools, unions and labor are considered resources or roadblocks to be manipulated, and business professors teach future and present executives how to do that. Few law schools teach lawyers how to ferret out and prosecute corporate crime, but they all teach lawyers how to defend business against such accusations.

One can also find a direct correlation in most universities and colleges, public and private, between the usefulness of a professor or an academic discipline to the business and governmental communities and the level of the professor's salary. The differences in rewards are justified by that old economic maxim which we are conditioned to believe without question is actually morally defensible: It's just a matter of supply and demand.

Our universities and colleges, on the whole, by the way they define the responsibilities of professors, are places to warehouse those who challenge the dominant view of reality. These "liberals" tend to reenforce our deep hopelessness. Most professors in the "liberal arts" are expected to analyze the products and structures of our society, and, as long as there is tenure, to critique them "appropriately." If students were hopeless about change before entering the university, these professors will show them how much worse things are by laying bare how systematic and entrenched our institutions, ideas, and symbols are.

Liberal arts professors in particular are not supposed to be involved personally in the issues they raise. They are to research them, observe them, analyze them, write about them and maintain an objectivity toward them. It is "appropriate" to study working class people or other non-dominant groups and their "lifestyles," but not to identify with them, their issues, or their movements. The profession itself has consistently looked down on actual involvement and activism by professors in fields which do not promote the goals of business and government, labeling it "unprofessional" and "unobjective."

Yet professors in the schools of engineering, business, management, law, and government are rewarded for their involvement and it is called "consulting." Business students train to become business people. Law students train to become lawyers. But humanities and social science graduates are traditionally trained to become professors, if they don't go into business, but not social activists.

Add to this popularly invoked images that attempt to dismiss the university as an ivory tower, the professor as so academically minded he or she is no earthly good, and higher education itself with the oft-repeated claim, both within and outside the institution, that it's not the "real world." Then reward professors for writing books to their academic colleagues with insider jargon so that their views are seldom accessible to the general public. As a result, the marginalization of liberal arts professors is complete. Finally, note that the ultimate justification we give for evaluating our colleges and universities is either the kind of employees they produce for American business, or how that education (actually "the degree," its product) will increase their graduates' salaries.

THE ISSUE REALLY IS "THE SYSTEM"

In fact, all of the institutions of our society have been working together to teach this view of reality from the very beginning. It has seldom been self-conscious. And educators and others have not been consciously and critically developing their curricula in these terms. But they too were raised in the same water, the same view of reality, the same values. So, our teachers began with the same basic assumptions about reality.

As we grew up, few of us questioned their assumptions. The teachings that constituted this view seemed to describe "just the way it is" because they came to us from every side, because our role models embodied them, and because there were no significant, visible exceptions. In fact, society's very definition of "growing up" meant that we had fully accepted these ideas and were learning to live in harmony with these institutions so that we would be "successful" in the institutions and they would "reward" us for it.

Together these institutions taught us about what was worthwhile and how we could be worthwhile. They taught us how to be "real" human beings, and how to be acceptable and loved. They taught us how to be "real" men, and how to be "real" women. And they all reinforced each other as a total system, what has been called "the system."

They most often worked together as efficiently as a healthy digestive system. The cultural system was not only the sum of its parts. It also included how the parts worked together to maintain the health of each institution. Just as the digestive system would not function if a stomach, pancreas, liver, and other organs were merely laid out before us on a table, so, our cultural system functions only when its institutions work together systematically to support each other and to train its members to constantly promote the health of the system.

In this way the ideas we learned were everywhere, not just in our formal education. The late twentieth-century family structure was supposed to embody these ideas. As the soldiers came home from Europe and Asia after 1945, we needed an ideal family which would make room for them by bringing "Rosie the Riveter" and other women out of the workplace and into the home or into "women's jobs." We needed a family ideal that would promote post-war prosperity.

Previously, many families were producing as well as consuming units. They not only purchased things from others for their own consumption but produced goods and services others would consume. They were households of more than two adults with many children who were tied to a family business, store, or farm. And the sons would often follow in their father's footsteps. This began to change earlier, but it would have to fade away as the need for peace-time consumption increased to replace somewhat the economy of war. The family had to be primarily a consuming unit. That unit was the nuclear family and it finally became the popular model. Few other relatives than dad, mom, and the children were needed in the home.

This nuclear form of the family would be justified by our religious institutions, as religious leaders searched in authorities such as the Bible for that rare model of a nuclear family. It was projected into the Bible in the same way slavery had been before. Since the Bible came out of traditional cultures, biblical families modeled polygamy and large households with relatives and servants in abundance, but the only apparent example of a nuclear family was one the biblical authors never themselves used as a model for the family, the story of Adam and Eve. This could be used to religiously justify the new model, and soon we would also begin to hear a new slogan to "protect" that family: "God created Adam and Eve, not Adam and Steve." The "traditional" family used in contemporary religious rhetoric, with the father as the bread winner and the mother as the homemaker, was blessed by religion, even though as a primary model it was far from traditional.

Our economic institutions, including Wall Street and Madison Avenue, promoted this view of reality as the key to financial success. The mushrooming advertising industry convinced us that we too can gain both success and the look of success through purchasing the products our industries needed to sell. Fulfillment was therefore more intensely measured by a conspicuous consumption. A successful life, we were taught, meant not mere security, not merely "keeping up with the Joneses," but being the "Joneses" people were supposed to admire. Contentment was out of the question for a growing economy.

Our dominant religious institutions added transcendent value to this view of reality we were learning. They often spoke of the system's ideals as divine decrees, interpreting old texts so that their scriptures taught the view, and finding the system's contemporary institutions in their authorized traditions in order to invoke them as models for today.

All in all, we were taught not to "rock the boat" and to be good consumers who would do what it takes to keep the economy booming. The other social institutions which we joined — clubs, teams, cliques, and societies — reinforced the dominant view. Openly embracing the ideas of the view was what allowed us to maintain our respectable memberships, and, as we know, "membership has its privileges."

When this systematic nature of our conditioning is the topic of discussion, some people ask: Isn't an institution, a corporation, or a school, just its people? A careful look, notices that it is more. An individual at a strategic place can make or break some institutions, but the institutions are not just the sum of individuals. In the process of their own development, institutions take on a life of their own beyond the particular human beings in them. Institutions last to the extent that they support the dominant view. They must conform to the dominant culture or be ridiculed, lose support, and die.

The individuals who belong to these institutions which reward them with economic "security" and culturally-determined worth are far from neutral and completely free agents who can effect, or even see the need for, structural change. First, the individuals had to qualify even before they were allowed to enter the institution. They had to give evidence that they would "enhance" the institution through the activities and attitudes which reflected how the institution had already defined "enhancement." They had to accept the direction set by the institution's official history or its current mythology. They had to fit somehow in the institution even before they were hired, accepted, or voted into place.

Once they joined the institution as employees or members, they had to regularly prove that they conformed to what has been called the "institutional culture" in order to be rewarded financially and to qualify for advancement to a place of effecting policy. There is no future for the one who does not show that she or he "fits." The deviant will not only fail to rise in the hierarchy of the institution but, more than likely, will experience a premature exit. If one wants rewards, she or he must become what came to be called a "company man." One must appear to have conquered the institution's culture, values, and goals and must be enforcing them on others. To do otherwise will result not only in the end of employment or advancement, but in ridicule from others as they judge the non-conformist inept, unable to do it, lazy, without drive, unambitious, deficient in talent, unable to cut it, unprofessional, or some other sort of failure in the game of life.

Of course, as we discuss the systemic nature of the view of reality, its pervasiveness and power, we also remember that we are talking about the variety of individuals that we are. We recognize that we are individuals who are personally in the water that is this way of seeing things we received. We are talking about the origins of our ideas, feelings, emotions, and responses in our childhoods. Yet people not only react in diverse ways to their cultural conditioning, they also take this conditioning and, mostly unconsciously, negotiate different scenarios of how to live it out in a variety of interactions. It is, after all, not destiny we received from our up-bringing, but conditioning. Though every person's childhood is different and there is as much variety in our pasts as there are people who tell of their stories, we each had to negotiate around and about some common themes as we grew up. We often knew these themes were there, even if we didn't embrace them. We knew we had to relate to them in some fashion, or suffer the consequences.

IDEAS, IMAGES, PENALTIES, AND FEAR

The power and depth of this view of reality is due first to the fact that our broader education was not a mere conceptual exercise. We learned not only of concepts, information, and theories, but we were shown images and symbols which we in turn embraced. These were images of the successful and admired man and woman, images which were burned into our psyches and thereby illustrated the dominant view. We were given images of "success" like Miss America, the chief executives of corporations, and military and sports heroes. We were also given images of failure, such as the sick, skid row bum, the helpless drug addict, the lonely, fragile, "old maid," and the patient dying alone in a "sterile" hospital, sick, friendless, and cold. We came to carry such images deeply. They pictured what we could become if we failed to master the system. And these images could be even more powerful than ideas, for "a picture is worth a thousand words."

Far more important for understanding why this view of

reality is so strong and deep is the fact that we did not learn the rules of the game merely by receiving factual information — or, I'd argue, misinformation — from these institutions. We were taught this view of reality and its definitions by experiencing ourselves, or observing others experiencing, the personal penalties suffered by anyone who did not embrace and live by the rules. The installation of the software was through emotional channels, not merely intellectual ones. And the penalties of rejecting the software were clear and fearful.

The software was installed in us through learning in early childhood what could happen to us if we "bucked the system" or "rocked that boat." It could be violence and physical, emotional, and psychological punishment. We could be hit by our parents or beaten by our peers. It could be the mere threat of violence. We noticed how people and institutions treated others who saw things differently and stepped out of the acceptable norms, and we didn't want that to happen to us. We learned that this violence could be economic as well. We could be denied the chance to earn a living or the basic economic means to obtain the necessities of life.

If we didn't accept and participate in the dominant view of reality, we could also receive ridicule and humiliation from the adults around us whose love and support we needed. As children we may have been criticized for acting "childish," we may have been shamed because we were not acting like a "little lady" or were being a "cry-baby."

From our peers we learned that acceptance meant we had to conform. Otherwise we were the one who was picked on by the group we valued, teased by the bully, and taunted by the other kids. Our peers learned the view quickly from the adults around them, and when children enforced it on each other, the adults labeled it "peer pressure." We may even have learned that if we did not participate in the enforcement of the view and its rules and norms on each other, we would be suspected of deviance and receive the same threats. We may have joined in, or even initiated, the teasing and taunting in order to be accepted.

The worst sanctions of all involved isolation and rejection. Those people whom we valued,who gave birth to us, or whom we sought out for love and acceptance, might reject us, abandon us, or isolate us from them. We did not want to be left alone. We wanted to belong to our families and to our groups of friends, and the cost of belonging was to pay the price of following the conditions society set.

The fear of being alone, was the worst fear of all. Adults today who are trying to heal their emotional lives still talk of their "abandonment issues." Fear of abandonment appears to be a wide-spread cultural hurt. This is no wonder, because abandonment was the strongest, most effective fear coming from all around us, always threatening if we did not conform.

Abuse would be better than isolation and rejection, for at least in abuse, there is some human contact, some assurance that we are not alone. For self-preservation, abused children return to the abuser for further abuse. Negative attention is better than being left alone without any human contact. When they are grown, however, survivors take the blame personally for returning to the abuser and "asking for it." From the perspective of survival, the abused child's rejection of isolation was the best strategy that a child who already felt alone in the abuse, without allies to protect it, could have developed. Isolation and rejection are fatal.

The fact that these were the methods of installing and maintaining the system's view of reality meant that our messages about what is moral and valuable, our comforting assumptions about "the way things are," our cultural teachings, our definitions of self and gender, and what we learned about the means we should use to conform to the rules of the game around us, in other words the elements of the software, were taught deeply to us not merely through education but through fear and even terror of what might happen if we didn't get it and live it well. Feelings were the method of making us get the point. And those feelings are there still.

This View of Reality Must Not Be Disturbed

I vividly remember strolling through many acres of a family farm with its owner, a close friend who would leave it behind in a few weeks, never to look back. The Kansas wheat was as golden as I'd ever seen it. The corn was "as high as an elephant's eye." The farm buildings and sheds were immaculate and even seemed to glow in the early evening sun. Steve was proud of his part of this legacy that he had inherited from his father and his father before him. And now it was time to move on to the relaxing life he had planned for at least a decade. He was really looking forward to "retiring," though I knew that he would never sit still.

As we walked, he began to cry. I had never seen the extent of these tears before. He told me story after story of the pain that went into that farm to make it one of the best in central Kansas. He confessed that he had not realized before what emotional effort he had invested in trying to make his farm what "a good farm should be." Even as a child working along side his parents, he remembered sacrifices in lean years, fears of seemingly impossible debts made almost annually, and the realization that the weather of the central plains is frighteningly unpredictable. The emotions that had been suppressed to make it through were now resurfacing as he gave up the lifestyle he had always known and faced a happy alternative.

In the same way, all of the emotions that installed the view of reality that we have tried to live by in our own lives are down there inside. So when someone challenges the point, threatens to rock the boat, or suggests alternatives to the dominant teachings and structures, our normal reaction is not merely one of relaxed curiosity and expectant learning. Anger, shouting, physical violence, sadness, tears, denial, or numbness, depending upon how we were conditioned to react, are likely as we feel the threat to our old ideas and re-feel the emotions that installed them. That's why the well-known saying of nineteenth century German philosopher Arthur Schopenhauer is so prophetic: "Every truth passes through three stages before it is recognized. In the first it is ridiculed, in the second it is opposed, in the third, it is accepted as self-evident."

We seldom see challenges to these core beliefs as welcome opportunities that we have been given to explore ourselves, our self-definitions, and the direction of our lives. The fear involved in the sanctions that installed the software and the accompanying sense that this was an offense to our wider, inborn, pre-conditioned humanity, reemerges. Our reactions arise from our hidden depths when someone touches the issues, questions them, or even points them out effectively. The same fears and hurts are re-engaged that were the means by which the software was installed. Our reaction is, therefore, most likely to be an emotional one.

In fact, we will marshal all the defenses we can to protect us from going through those negative feelings once more. We will protect ourselves (actually the image and definitions we have been given of ourselves as part of the culture's view of reality) as if examining the alternatives to the current view means that even we, in the process, will be abandoning our very selves. It will raise the fear that without these definitions we will not know who we are. The abandonment issues will be front and center.

It feels easier to fight back and protect the definitions that we have accepted of who we are and who others are. We may not be ready to step out into the unknown frontier and feel those emotions that taught us deeply the lessons of our institutions. That would appear to be stepping out alone, isolated, and rejected.

The installation of our culture's view of reality into us, then, is deep and heartfelt. This is because, beginning at birth, it came from everywhere. It is because the conditioning included images as well as intellectual concepts, and because it was installed emotionally, not just intellectually. The key emotions that installed the software were fear, and even terror, of the consequences of rejecting the dominant view. We proved we accepted it by passing the view along and enforcing it on others. And the measure of the fear involved in its installation is the variety and intricacy of the contortions we go through not to feel those feelings again.

We don't want the renewed discomfort we would feel when the core issues are resurrected. Yet, raising the issues, examining them and feeling the corresponding emotions again is a positive move because we are now adults who can afford to feel them. We can now realize that when we feel them today the emotions and fears are coming out, not going in.

Transgendered and bisexual people and gay men and lesbians are discriminated against because their deviation from a societal norm raises these core fears in us. It involves phobia. So we have to work on our fears, search them out, identify them, recognize their origins, and move past them, if we merely want to understand these issues. No matter what our sexual orientation is, we have fear work to do in order to accept gay people, and, more importantly, to accept ourselves. First, we need to take a closer look at the conditioning that installed one of the very basic fears in our view of reality, a fear we have come to call "homo-phobia."

Further Reading

John Taylor Gatto, *Dumbing Us Down: The Hidden Curriculum of Compulsory Schooling.* Gabriola Island, BC: New Society Publishers, 1991.

Paul Rogat Loeb, *Soul of a Citizen: Living with Conviction in a Cynical Time.* New York: St. Martin's Griffin, 1999.

Alice Miller, *For Your Own Good: Hidden Cruelty in Child-rearing and the Roots of Violence.* New York: Noonday Press, 1990.

Alice Miller, *Thou Shalt Not be Aware: Society's Betrayal of the Child.* New York: Noonday Press, 1998.

Howard Zinn, *A People's History of the United States: 1492 to the Present.* New York: Harper Perennial, 1995.

CHAPTER THREE

Is It Pink or Is It Blue?

What does all of this have to do with society's attitudes toward gay, lesbian, bisexual, and transgendered people? To answer that question, we need to examine the dominant pattern of conditioning that the system installs in us, particularly as it relates to a cultural value called "homophobia."

We hear people define the term "homophobia" in a variety of ways. Often it is used as a general label for attitudes which might better be labeled ignorance, hatred, or prejudice. Yet, there is one definition which does get to the cultural foundation of all the other issues labeled "homophobia." In order to understand more fully the interworkings of our cultural system and to penetrate behind our difficulties with fully accepting the variety of sexual orientations, it's important to examine our own culture's conditioning by using this more basic definition.

At its most basic level, then, homophobia is the fear of getting close to one's own sex. Obviously, that refers to a variety of male fears about getting too close to other males and a variety of female fears about becoming too close to other females.

"Phobia" is the appropriate designation for this conditioning because homophobia itself, first, is an emotional fear that is installed by the systemic conditioning. Second, this homophobia is installed by means of fear — fear of violence and threats of violence, ridicule, rejection, and abandonment. Third, the same fears that installed the fear of closeness to one's own sex are the primary emotions which sooner or later arise when a person feels she or he has become "too close" to a member of the same sex. In other words, fear is the content of homophobia, fear installs and maintains it, and fear again arises when homophobia is challenged.

Homophobia in this basic sense is a conditioned response, an approach to life, a learned attitude, which plays a crucial role in the view of reality that is dominant in the institutions of our culture. For example, homophobia supports our market economy. If people are afraid to feel and express a natural human closeness, it is easier to sell them all sorts of products by promising that using these products will bring feelings of closeness. So, Madison Avenue advertises almost every product with the claim that it will bring love, closeness, and acceptance. Tires, automobiles, deodorant, the right home, the perfect gift, and the tastiest food are all sold with the images and promise that people will like us, admire us, or desire us better if we indulge in them. These purchases will finally enable us to break through the barriers to acceptance and love.

In our most reflective moments we notice that this promise, of course, is illusory. Since nothing can substitute for the unconditional, natural human closeness we seek to recover and which homophobia as the fear of closeness with half the human species removes, we ultimately understand, and sometimes even confess, that we cannot buy closeness. The conditioning, therefore, promises what it can't deliver to us while it guarantees what our economy needs, an unabated market for these products.

Even so, homophobia is a cultural condition, a major chemical found in the water that surrounds us. It is a conditioned characteristic of everyone regardless of sexual orientation. Essentially it has nothing to do with sexual orientation. Yet prejudices about, and discrimination and violence toward, people perceived to be homosexual is a direct result of this conditioning because the existence and visibility of gay, lesbian, bisexual and transgendered people embodies the fear itself. They seem to contradict the homophobia. And focusing on them is a way to take our attention off of our deep, systematic fear so we won't feel the fear that installed it again or won't have to admit we are actually afraid.

We will discuss how this conditioned homophobia actually effects people in later chapters. First, though, let's examine the process by which this particular fear was deeply installed.

Surprisingly, homophobia actually has more to do with something other than issues of sexual orientation. In fact, homophobia hurts all of us because it has more to do with societally conditioned definitions of "masculinity" and "femininity." The definitions of manhood and womanhood homophobia enforces actually strip from us much of who we are as complete human beings, leaving us only with quite limiting gender roles by which to define ourselves. I want to point out in the process of this discussion that oppression, prejudice, and discrimination directed toward gay people are in reality the means for installing, maintaining, enforcing, and valuing gender roles, which are our conditioned definitions of what a "real" man or woman is in our society.

Let's take an honest look at the general patterns of our own up-bringing. Let's ask ourselves which of the following we experienced directly or indirectly. Ask which you were aware of as it took place around you, but was not a part of your personal experience. Did you see this going on with others and learn from those observations to watch your behavior, to focus attention on those others, to keep silent, or to develop and carefully monitor your own lifestyle so as to skirt the conditioning? Watch closely how you react as you read what is on the following pages. What do you do emotionally to deal with the fact that this conditioning actually came at you personally through fear of the consequences of not accepting or colluding with it? Where do you go emotionally so as not to feel any fear again?

SEARCHING FOR CAUSES THAT WON'T DISRUPT THE STATUS QUO

We are at a time in history when it is popular to seek genetic causes for most human traits. The pressure, for example, is to show that men are inherently, biologically, or genetically violent, or rapists, or aggressive, or hyper-sexual, and women inherently, biologically, or genetically more nurturing and submissive. There is considerable research money available for those interested in such pursuits. If we can find genetic, chemical, or non-social causes for human issues, we can put our hope in medication, therapeutic drugs, and scientific engineering of some sort as "solutions" to social problems. Pharmaceutical and surgical solutions provide customers for pharmaceutical and health care corporations as well, bolstering the economic system. Finding these "solutions" is easier and more lucrative for business than focusing on causes that require us to face our individual fears and to make major changes in societal attitudes and institutions. If a Hallmark card can't solve your relationship problems, how about a Zanax? So, the search for genetic and medicinal causes is a search for solutions that promote the current view of reality, while providing the hope that cures are available for purchase. Science, like religion, has often been at the service of the dominant structures, so this should not surprise us.

We can also read those scholars who argue for sociobiological explanations for differences in male and female behavior. They conclude that these differences are stubbornly, even hopelessly, inherent to each sex. It is, more popular writers claim, as if men and women come from planets as different as Mars and Venus.

Such academic theories speculate that gender differences are the result of adaptations to the long history of human evolution in response to our physical and social environments. One version attempts to explain differences by theorizing that it was to the male's advantage to "spread his genes." That's why males came to devote a larger portion of their mating efforts to short-term relationships, whereas women benefitted from long-term mating.

These theories neglect the more likely fact that there was historical diversity in human environments, not one single pattern for all human development. In reality, though, these theories are actually backward predictions. They lack any clear evidence from the past. They take our current gender roles and look back to find explanations for them by guessing that the differences must be adaptations to the long history of environmental and evolutionary conditions we humans have had to face. Even if we were to grant that some of these differing characteristics were a result of evolution, if they no longer serve us, it's time to move beyond them. But more importantly, these theories actually fail to explain the evidence we do have. They do not help us understand the current differences in gender roles we can observe across cultures. In the long run, these attempts aren't helpful, much less verifiable.

Not surprisingly, then, there are numerous claims in the popular media today that the gender differences between boys and girls are "hard wired" or genetic, not taught. To illustrate this claim we often hear references to studies of four or five year old children. The more popular books and articles often present these studies without the cautions of the actual researchers, and, at times, the results are actually misread in these popular presentations.

Frankly, these studies of early childhood are not at all helpful in proving genetic origins. Instead, they actually illustrate that by an early age gender conditioning has already taken hold. By then children have been conditioned relentlessly during all their waking hours in all their social environments for those four or five years.

There are numerous research studies which support the following scenario of gender conditioning I'm about to rehearse. In the last thirty-five years children and gender have been researched extensively. These controlled studies that have been done with children from birth are in mind as we take another look at the conditioning children undergo as they grow up in the United States.

KNOWING WHAT THIS BABY IS

Our general survey begins with a child's birth. There are some suggestions that we ought to begin earlier, but let's start with the first moment a child sees daylight.

When a baby is born, the first question adults ask is something like: "What is it?" If we were to answer that this is "a human being," that would almost universally be considered an insufficient answer and even beside the point. Something in the adult's own well-conditioned view of reality compels them to know: "Is it a boy or a girl?" Is it to be wrapped in pink or blue, for in recent times pink has become a color for females. At the beginning of the twentieth century, the conditioning said just the opposite: pink was too garish for women. Black was much more "appropriate." But the conditioning we receive from our culture today convinced us that certain colors are naturally related to only one of the sexes.

This compulsion to know the sex of a new human being tells us that adults can't relate to the baby as a full, open human being with all human possibilities ahead of it. In order to understand and react to the child, conditioned adults just have to know it's sex.

With my undergraduate college students who are already quite familiar with gender issues, I have shared a story by Lois Gould, entitled "X: A Fabulous Child's Story." It's a fantasy that tells of two parents who raise a young person without telling the child its sex. When asked, the parents respond not by say-ing it's a boy or girl but that it's an "X." As we discuss the story in class, students express their own frustration with not know-ing. Some just dismiss the story as unbelievable. I tell them to look at it again as just a fantasy and to try to step outside their conditioning to imagine what this would be like. Some women assume "X" must be a boy because of "X's" "freedom." Some students believe that not telling the child is cruel and harmful. "X" needs to know, they say. The child's parents respond to questions about when they will tell "X" its gender by: "We'll tell 'X' when 'X' needs to know." That answer is not good enough for some of my students. They feel that "X" must know when it is time to find a sexual partner. I then ask, why even then? Can't the young person fall in love with whomever it wants?

Their frustration with the story, which is common, indi-cates that they have difficulty even fantasizing about the pos-sibility of living without the limitations "X" would have if "X" were given a gender idea with which to conform. The depth of that frustration and their difficulty merely allowing the possi-bility of an alternative into their minds, indicates not only how deeply we have been conditioned, but also how thoroughly and unconsciously we are conditioning our children from the moment they are born.

Try not asking the question of sex when you hear that a new baby has been born. Notice, first, how incomplete you yourself might feel for not asking, as if you had broken some major rule of etiquette. Then, see if your failure to ask about the sex of the child is interpreted by other adults as meaning that you lack interest in the human being that has just been born or in its parents, or that you are just unwilling to share the parents' "joy." Is it interpreted as a lack of desire to inter-act with the new born?

Now, the baby is not asking the question of sex: "Tell me, adults, what I am, so I know how to live my life and how to be a baby." The baby seems to relate to the world about it in terms of its full humanity. Even Sigmund Freud, whose psycho-analytic theories often justified conditioned gender differences, recognized that boys and girls are all alike in what he called their first psycho-sexual developmental stages.

From birth on, though, the system uses every means at its disposal to internalize a gender identity into the child. We know, for example, that parents and other adults interact differently through speech and emotions with boys than with girls, often unconsciously so. They express their relationship physically differently with each through how they play and cuddle. They expect different behaviors from each. They provide different toys to boys and girls. Studies show that little boys are more likely to be handled roughly, wrestled with, encouraged to play aggressively, and punished physically. Girls are taught to stand back and show timidity, consideration for others, and emotional sensitivity.

The system teaches us through example and training to take human qualities which are shared by both sexes and to divide them between boys and girls. It denies some human qualities to each sex and enforces them on the other. Parents, grandparents, peers, and the media are concerned that boys will be boys and girls will learn to be girls. As the old nursery rhyme put it: "Snips, and snails, and puppy dog's tails" for one, while "sugar and spice and everything nice" belong to the other. There are "masculine" qualities and "feminine" qualities. Even adults who are trying to explore alternatives to their own conditioning still often speak in these terms by talking about getting in touch with their "masculine" or "feminine" sides.

Before they enter school, children show that they have already learned that maleness equates with competitiveness, dominance over others, self-reliance, and always appearing tough. It means being a talker more than a listener, displaying self-confidence, valuing abstract thinking, and being a quick decision maker. The games young boys are taught to play, researchers have noted, involve more competition than those for young girls. Even recent research in the light of the increase of women's sports still shows this difference in competition. No wonder it will become hard for men to ask others for help or directions when they are lost, and it will be a source of stress when they are forced to do so. It's a matter of living up to a role that must win.

The conditioning defines "femininity," on the other hand, to involve submission, emotional expression, dependency, vulnerability, quietness, and looking and being "pretty." "Sitting there like a little lady," is a phrase that immediately brings this image to mind. Women are expected to need and ask for help, particularly from men, who, in turn, are expected to be able to help in order to avoid questioning their own manhood.

Little children pay close attention. From the beginning and like sponges, they observe, imitate, and categorize themselves by soaking up adult attitudes and understandings. Boys and girls both learn what the "man" is in the house, while they see the model of a "woman." The real "advantage" of a two-parent household with both a father and a mother is that it provides both models of fully conditioned gender roles for children.

Children hear phrases such as "girls play with dolls," and "boys play with trucks." And the media advertise in these terms. As I write this I have on my desk an advertisement from Mattel for two "Real Computers Designed Just for Kids." One is trimmed in pink with flowers and called the "Barbie" computer. The other is blue, trimmed in yellow flames, and called the "Hot Wheels" computer. The accompanying "20 software titles" that come with each are "appropriately" different to enforce the gender roles.

LEARNING WHAT TO DO WITH OUR EMOTIONS

Society also teaches each sex to deal differently with their natural human emotions. Remember, however, that these appropriate male and female reactions are taught not merely by giving people information but through the fear of what will happen to a girl or boy if she or he does not react "appropriately" for their defined gender.

There are two layers of conditioning that take place regarding emotions. The first is the *content* of the conditioning. This teaches a girl or a boy with what emotions each should react to life's circumstances in order to be reacting the way a "real" woman or a "real" man should. Real girls react one way and real boys react another. They react by having the emotions in the learned manner. The second layer is the actual fear-based *application* or installation of the gender "appropriate," conditioned emotional reactions to replace the initial, unconditioned emotional reactions themselves, "appropriate" or "inappropriate." On the first layer, the boy or girl learns the appropriate reactions for actually having the emotions, that is, how to respond to them. They are to respond to emotions women or men are not supposed to have by flipping into conditioned female or male reactions to these emotions. On the second layer she or he reacts to the method of learning how to react as a real man or woman, that is to the fear by which the "appropriate" reactions were learned. Both boys and girls not only are hurt, but they may also have gotten hurt for expressing their hurt. "I'll give you something to cry about," may have been said. A boy, for example, is taught first not to feel hurt. He is also taught to deny the hurt involved in being taught this. A girl is taught that she shouldn't feel angry. And she is taught that she shouldn't be angry for being taught this! There is something wrong with *her* if she feels her anger.

This conditioning denies boys in particular the freedom to express fears not sanctioned by, and useful to, the system. A man might hesitantly admit some fear in war, where men are officially killing other men, as long as these men do not act upon the fear. They are therefore labeled cowards for dodging the draft even though that is an act taken against all the consequences. Fears that are not "official" but personal are taboo.

This is part of that second layer of hurt that is added on top of the first. By means of fear itself — fear of punishment, threats of violence, ridicule and abandonment, boys are taught to react to fear "like a man." Therefore they are also taught not to admit experiencing the fearful process that taught them how to react to fear, hurt and confusion. Even to face this process in his life would be to face the fear they cannot let in. "My parents hit me, and I turned out all right," a conditioned adult can bravely say.

The need to control and deny emotions is, of course, exaggerated for boys, while feminine "emotionality" is expected, encouraged, and then demeaned. Real men are always supposed to be in control. That includes being in control of their emotions. Boys are taught to believe they should not cry and should be very limited in the expression of their emotions. Being stoic is taught early. "Don't be a crybaby" may be repeated, or "only girls cry," or "big boys don't cry" (installing also the idea that bigger is better). The result is that boys soon understand that their masculinity is on the line when they express fear or hurt.

This conditioning of men to deny that they have hurts puts men out of touch with the fact that they are actually being hurt. "Does that bother you?" might be his response to another's expression of hurt, pain or concern, as if the man is surprised that something actually does bother anyone. He clearly implies that whatever it is, it shouldn't bother real men, while he puts down anyone who does express these natural feelings, whether they be male or female.

A man conditioned to be out of touch with his own feelings of hurt also finds it harder to believe that he is actually hurting others. This makes it easier for a well-conditioned man to hurt others both personally and through sexism, racism, and classism, while not believing he is doing so. William Pollack, a Harvard Medical School professor and researcher, has concluded that the shame boys are taught to experience just for having feelings that are labeled "feminine," is "the primary or ultimate cause of all violence, whether toward others or toward the self."

Men are not inherently this way. They have to be "carefully taught," as the song from the musical "South Pacific" goes. And it must be a regular, sustained, and painful education, for they have to be taught through fear of the consequences.

In fifth grade, my son wanted to join an organized "little league" football team. I was not thrilled, for I had heard my colleagues in the Department of Health, Physical Education and Recreation argue, against the dominant football establishment, that it was a sport that should be put off until long bone development was completed. He really wanted to play, and I agreed. At the first game my not-yet-thoroughly-conditioned son came up to me in full uniform to explain something that had not yet been taught in his view of reality. "Dad, dad," he said. "The coach is going to tell us to kill the other team, but he doesn't really mean it." He had not yet learned that "teamwork" for conditioned males meant men getting together to beat, defeat, hurt, and kill another group of males, often literally.

Boys will soon learn that real men are also decisive, forward thinking, and sure of themselves. The right to change one's mind is a quality for girls. Real men must move forward, unflinching, even if it hurts. They must always appear to be in charge, never appearing to abandon a course of action, even if they begin to feel they are on the wrong one. And the longer they are on that course, the harder it will be to change, for that would be understood as an admission that they did not know, were not in control, or had just plain "failed." Instead, the more energy, effort, time, and stress conditioned men have invested in the course, the more they will need to deny the error of the course, or the harder they will work to make it positive and to reward those who join them on it.

Denial is an important tool to save manhood. What man who has gone off to fight in a war and made all the sacrifices of his in-born humanity that war entails, personally experiencing something like the first gruesome thirty minutes of the movie *Saving Private Ryan*, will be able to admit without serious mental anguish that he might have fought it in vain? America's Viet Nam experience, which even then Secretary of Defense Robert MacNamara now admits was a terrible error, still illustrates this. Depression, addictions, mental illness, denial, and suicide, have been the coping mechanisms for many of these men.

Boys and men are not supposed to stop to ask for directions. That would evidence confusion and inability. If they do have to change course, someone else must be at fault. The real man is a leader, illustrated by the orchestrated public image of President Ronald Reagan. He was portrayed as a man who never had to change his mind and always was on track. President Bill Clinton's policy of negotiating, listening to the opinions of others, considering various responses, and adjusting to new information, even changing his mind after hearing a good argument, has been criticized as weak leadership. President Clinton's leadership style of consideration and nuance of thought was questioned as "unmanly." One of the pressures to look decisive, particularly in war, is the need to appear "manly." It is a typical male criticism to say: "Women are always changing their minds." Real men know where they are going in life and are "on track." And the best men know this early.

NO FEAR, HURT, OR CONFUSION HERE

Male gender conditioning soon teaches boys how to "deal" with emotions that "real men" don't express directly. In fact, they usually learn that they shouldn't even admit to having fear, hurt, and confusion at all. "Deal" may actually be a poor choice of words for the conditioned male process. To "deal" with emotions would mean to recognize them, feel them, and work though the issues they entail. But the conditioning installs the means of "dealing" with these three emotions so deep that male reactions become amazingly quick, automatic, and unconscious. It takes quite a bit of reflection and safety from judgment for anyone to face what is really happening. When fear, hurt, or confusion do threaten, as they do in all human beings, successfully conditioned men have been taught to react to these "negative" emotions in three particular ways which are acceptable for the manhood role.

First a boy is conditioned to minimize these emotions. This is taught at almost every opportunity by both fathers and mothers, and especially on the athletic field. As a result he may minimize them personally with: "They weren't that bad." Or, looking back on his childhood, he might use some version of: "They helped me become a man." But most often they are minimized by labeling them "baby stuff" or "feminine." "Only babies cry" and "Only girls cry," go together as minimizations, and both adults and peers will say so. Society allows "girls" to express these "negative" emotions, but they are put down for doing so.

Any thing, idea, person, or image that threatens one's masculinity, that raises the fear that a man is not masculine enough, can be minimized. I am reminded of a common response of college men I have known when they are confronted by the models of consumer masculinity in clothing catalogues such as *Undergear, International Male,* or *GQ.* These high-paid models might spend about a third of their life working on their sculpted looks and another third with the photographers who must get the lighting, airbrushing, and computer enhancing just right on thousands of photos to find the one that will make the models look like "perfect specimens." When everyday men compare their own average appearance to these models, it can be quite threatening, for they see themselves in competition with each other and even with these models, particularly for female attention. A conditioned male can't admit the threat. It's too much like fear and failure. So, a minimizing response is to say: "Oh, they're probably all gay anyway." That is, they are not real men. So (sigh of relief here) women couldn't want them.

A second conditioned response to feelings men are taught to deny is isolation. There are numerous ways to isolate. It's common to expect men to isolate in an addiction. In fact, it is often assumed that when men say they are in a "support group," the group is sponsored by Alcoholics Anonymous or Sexual Addicts Anonymous or that it is another group intended to help men recover from addictions. When I have spoken about groups for dealing with men's issues, I have often been met with the question, "Do men have issues?" Or else I can tell that the assumption is that the group must be dealing with addictions.

Workaholism is the most common, recognized, but minimized, addiction because we have made it a necessary addiction for most of our institutions to function. Although it is functional for the system, it is probably as dysfunctional for the personal health of individuals as alcoholism or drug addiction. Channel surfing, use of alcohol or other drugs, much playing and watching sports, and even heady religion and correct theology, can be means men use to isolate from their feelings.

Women often observe another form of isolation conditioned to be so automatic in men that men honestly deny they experience this form of isolation. It takes someone from outside this particular male conditioning to notice it.

A woman might be having a relaxed, pleasant dinner with a good male friend or partner when suddenly she feels as if the man is no longer really there with her. She knows he is there bodily, but she senses he does not seem to be fully present. Something about him is elsewhere. He'll deny this, of course. If she quizzes him about this apparent emotional absence, he might respond that she is mistaken, that all is well, and that he is really listening. He might even get angry with her for suggesting he was not listening, not doing his duty as a man. Later, however, she may catch him having "forgotten" a conversation.

Something in the immediate environment — a word spoken, a stray thought, remembrance of some comment or event that questioned his competency earlier at work, a smell, or a familiar or challenging sight — had triggered feelings that he must not feel. He may add to his denial the minimization of his friend's or partner's suspicion by criticizing or satirizing "women's intuition" for suggesting he was not there for that moment. In reality, though, her feelings were accurate.

Boys also learn that there are rewards for being emotionally isolated from their bodily hurts. The real male hero "plays hurt." He plays with an injury, ignoring the messages of his body. There is little place for feeling hurt, fear, or confusion on the athletic field or the field of battle. Men are even rewarded for minimizing any pain and isolating from their bodies. What a role model such real men are. "Did you see that touchdown run? And he did it with two broken legs and a concussion. What a hero!" Appropriately, in the movie *Varsity Blues* the football coach tells his exhausted and hurting players, "The only pain that counts is the pain you inflict."

On a segment of PBS's "All Things Considered" years ago which discussed an American manufacturing firm whose goal was to put women at every level of its structure, the reporter interviewed a man who worked on the company's loading dock. In fact, he had worked on that dock for decades. "Yes," he said, "we had a woman working here, but she couldn't hack it. She just wasn't physically up to the pressure." It never occurred to him that he was out of touch with his body and apparently less healthy than the woman who left the dock. Instead his conditioned male reaction combined masculine isolation from his body with the minimizing of a woman for being in touch with her body: "I've been working on this dock for over twenty years. I've gone home with a splitting headache every day." He could take it, and he was proud of it. Not surprisingly men, physicians tell us, are more likely to ignore the signs their body gives them until it is too late.

One of the most common conditioned forms of male isolation from fear, hurt, and confusion, is to flip into an emotion which is considered appropriate for men: anger. In almost all cases, anger is a secondary emotion which is more acceptable for men (in most cases, as long as it is "controlled") than the primary emotions of fear, hurt, and confusion. So much is this the case that "anger management" has become popular as a means to cope with male anger.

I now begin with the assumption that all male anger is secondary, a statement that feelings of hurt, confusion, and fear have threatened to surface. "I am angry at you or what you said" may actually mean:

- "What you said made me feel like a little boy again."
- "What you said made me feel as if I weren't being taken seriously."
- "Were you trying to make a fool of me?"
- "What you said made me feel I was dumb."
- "What you said sounded like you were going to leave me, so I'll isolate from you first."
- "What you said made me feel as if you were questioning my masculinity."
- "What you did made me feel ashamed."
- "I am hurting and I want you to feel my anger to show you how bad I feel, since I can't tell you and still be a man."

After all the conditioning, what man can actually speak about, or even know at first, what his anger means without questioning the "manhood" role he was conditioned to embody?

A third conditioned male reaction to feelings of fear, hurt, and confusion, is abstraction. Our culture trains men to think in terms of the principle, the precedent, the law, the formula, the theory, or the rules. Abstracting from forbidden feelings can even take place when men gather in a men's support group where topics and issues are discussed and debated quite intellectually and analytically so that feelings are not felt around these other men.

Remember the 1960's situation comedy, "All in the Family"? Archie Bunker was predictably impatient with his wife Edith when she told stories in her own full and complete manner. He cajoled her over and over to get to some "point," putting her down all the way for indulging in all the details that for her brought the story itself to life.

Counselors tell us that retelling a story slowly with all its details, feelings, colors, smells, and impressions does bring the story "to life." It enables us to get to the feelings involved in the incident so that we can heal from our past hurts. Abstraction moves us further from the possibility of getting in touch with the emotions that installed any early neuroses. If you don't want to feel, "the devil is surely in the details." Principles, like math, are unfeeling. So they make good places to hide from emotions men should not feel.

When an eldest son, the one on whom the parents have placed so many expectations, reveals to his parents that he is gay, which parent do you expect is more likely to be the one conditioned to uphold the principle and the ethics, and which is more likely to say, "But he's our son"? Of course, this is not always the case, but you know which parent you identify with each reaction.

Which is more likely to think in terms of the individuals involved in specific incidents and relationships and their feelings — the gender that is conditioned to abstract in principles and laws or the gender allowed to feel the emotional, relational connection with the gay son? Who is more likely to value cold reasoning and hard thinking, no matter how human beings will be negatively effected by the results of that reasoning? The principle must be upheld, for that is what is supposed to be best for the system "in the long run," a man might believe. And he may even do this at the same time that he is feeling deep within that he does not want to do so. He is conditioned to believe this is his best strategy as a man, and the best way to make his son a man.

A successfully conditioned man is well-trained to abstract away from his feelings and to criticize women for the sympathy their conditioning allows them to feel and show. He is taught to minimize the feelings that are obvious in her reactions. This may aid boys to have a better math ability, while it conditions them how to respond when they do feel hurt, fear, or confusion. The difference in conditioning even affects how we communicate, as communication expert Deborah Tannen and others have observed. Men speak in terms of competition and hierarchy, women in terms of relationships and empathy.

"GIRLS ARE MORE EMOTIONAL, POOR THINGS"

Girls are permitted a wider variety of emotional expression and then they are minimized for having these emotions even if they do not openly express them. Almost universally, psychologists tell us that the ability to embrace and express one's emotions is psychologically healthier. Yet, because masculinity dominates our society, women's emotional expressions, and even the fact that they have emotions at all, are criticized.

In addition, since women are supposed to be submissive and responsive to men and their values, women's conditioned responses to feelings they are not supposed to have are, in reality, responses to male conditioning. Women are allowed to feel hurt, confusion and fear, because they are conditioned to rely on men to take care of these emotions. One emotion is, however, the glaring exception. Women are not to be angry.

Girls soon learn through the conditioning that there are "feminine" ways to deal with their emotions which are installed through fear of similar sanctions as those for boys. And these methods often become so automatic that they seem like second nature. They learn that their "femininity" and attractiveness to men are on the line if they should respond outside the conditioning, particularly through anger. There are special words for women who are angry, and they aren't "forceful, determined, passionate, focused, decisive, righteous, or strong."

First, since the dominant cultural view is to minimize emotions, the conditioning teaches women to devalue their natural emotional responses. These natural emotions are considered less helpful than cold, hard reasoning, than the abstraction in which men hide. The conditioning says that women's feelings can be useful for what we are conditioned to believe are "less important," that is women's, activities such as nurturing children, responding to affectionate advances, decorating the home, designing a flower garden, or choosing non-essential furnishings for the home. But they are not considered helpful for "really important" tasks like running a government, fighting a war, building an industry, securing greater profits, and "bringing home the bacon."

As women enter fields dominated by men, they will have to prove that they are as cold and reasoning as men. Or they will have to change the system to one that is less cold and reasoning and, in the process, face further criticism, marginalization, and lack of conditioned male acceptance for doing so. Either way, they will be criticized for not being "real women." They will be criticized for "emasculating" the system, that is making it less than conditioned masculinity. He, on the other hand, is an "Officer and a Gentleman."

Women are likely to take this further than merely devaluing their emotions, for women are even conditioned to believe that their feelings actually have no validity at all. Their feelings have little place, if any, and they don't help them understand reality at all — remembering that this "reality" is the particular "view of reality" installed in us by the system. What she feels tells us nothing when compared to reason. Her intuitions are useless. When she has them, no one should rely on them.

On top of this, if the conditioning is especially negative, women are meant to rely on men to save them from, or to properly interpret, their feelings. The "strong, silent type" of man often portrayed as the ideal, is the prince who in his decisive, rational, steeled manner, can save the heroine from the perils she falls into due to her "feminine" emotions and her other "feminine" weaknesses.

Second, society conditions women to transfer their unacceptable emotions, especially those of anger, to feelings that are acceptable for women. This transfer can become as automatic as men isolating from their feelings in anger. Women often cry tears of anger instead of expressing anger, or tears of joy, instead of breaking out in the hearty laughter acceptable for males. The poem "Anger," by Mahrya Monson, expresses this well.

Women are denied the release of swearing,
The fist driven through the wall,
Reverberations echoing through the neighborhood.
Sometimes we are allowed to slam doors.

When we were children,
We were told,
    "Don't be angry."
    "It's not nice to be angry."
Is that why
ANGER
GIVES ME A STOMACHACHE
MAKES ME
SHAKE
CAUSES ME TO FEEL
SICK?
I have often shed tears in anger.
Is that a more acceptable way
          for a
Woman
      to be
A*N*G*R*Y!?

This transfer of emotions confuses everyone. Women have reasons to be angry, but when they express it they often feel guilty. And men do not realize, or don't often want to know, the amount of rage that is deep inside women because women have been taught to hold it in.

Women themselves may be unable to get in touch with their anger easily, for it has been stuffed down, held in, and saved up for so long. To face it is to fly in the face of all their conditioning about womanhood. Yet, it must be expressed in safe settings before women too can get to the hurts they have suffered, both personally and through being minimized as human beings in a society that is male-dominated. If, as one psychologist has said, behind all depression is rage, I wonder how much anger needs expression to free women from their depression.

Men are afraid of women's anger, though they may not be able to admit their fear. They have a stake in denying women the expression of anger and they have not been taught how to deal with women's anger except through their own anger.

A woman who shows her anger to a man often reduces the man to feelings of being a victim. He feels like that little boy again who was punished by a female authority figure, usually a mother or a teacher. The emotions which women's anger raises cannot be felt by the man who needs to maintain his conditioned manhood. He must stop those feelings, and a flood of anger in return is the most "manly" way to do so. He is angry for feeling that he is a victim of women. A conditioned man must never admit to feeling that way.

A third conditioned response for women's emotions is also isolation. This is more likely to be a thorough "shutting down," sometimes physically as well as psychologically. It can result in out-of-body experiences like those expressed by people who have been abused physically or sexually. One becomes an observer of what is happening in one's own life and all that is around it. "I watched myself do my duty as a wife," one woman told me. "It was as if I were a third party observing someone else, even though I knew it was me." The goal is to leave the emotions if one cannot leave the scene.

Like conditioned male isolation, this too may result in addictions, but it can also be a flight into being the best victim possible, the best "little woman" one can be. Justifying the conditioned woman's role is a means of isolating from her emotions, and a conditioned response is to find a man to take her "negative" emotions away, to save her from feelings of isolation, rejection, and hurt, and to make her happy. She needs a "boyfriend" or a "husband" to rescue her.

PAYING ATTENTION TO EMOTIONS

Much more has been written about these conditioned gender responses to emotions. Not only were our roles installed through our emotions, but we were taught how to deal with those emotions on the basis of these same gender roles. The appropriate responses to the feelings were divided between boys and girls with girls allowed a wider variety of emotions. Though we were all born with the full range of human emotions, we soon came to know how we would be treated if we expressed those that were inappropriate to the conditioned role society wanted us to fill. So, the systemic conditioning not only denied our full humanity through these limiting roles, but also threatened us with a range of mistreatment if we chose to step out of those roles or express any real, heartfelt displeasure with them.

How we are conditioned to "deal" with our emotions is an important consideration for our discussion because it was by these emotions that our roles were installed, which include our homophobia. As we discuss the topic, we touch not only on the misinformation we were given, but on the feelings which installed our views. As we touch those emotions, they are bound to arise again. And we will find ourselves, if we are paying attention to our reactions to this book, experiencing the above responses we were conditioned to experience when feelings men or women are not supposed to have threaten to surface.

We need to practice an awareness that goes beyond gaining new information. We need to ask ourselves: Am I reacting by abstracting away from those feelings? Am I minimizing the author or speaker and the material to disengage from it? Is anger arising in me as I read this? Have I shut down my emotions completely?

Women, of course, have every right to be angry about what is written here. If men do not go into abstraction and minimization, they too have every right to get angry about what the conditioning denied them. They also need to get through the anger to the hurt and fear at the base of that anger.

Will women shut their own anger down by pitying men's conditioning? At the end of workshops I lead in which both women and men are in attendance, I ask each participant to list one thing that struck them anew, one thing that they learned, or just one thing they liked about the day. I force myself not to "teach" anything more at the time but to listen and give undivided attention. As a well-conditioned male and professional teacher, my temptation is to "straighten things out," teach some more, and rescue people during this closing exercise. I do not. Yet, I have noticed that only a few women respond to this request by saying how angry this makes them feel for the variety of reasons they deserve to be angry. More often they say that they learned how difficult it must be for men in our society, and they say this with a genuine feeling of empathy. It took almost eight years of workshops before I had a man say that he had realized how difficult it must be for women in our society. And that was the only one who has done so to date.

Now, there could be many reasons for this difference in response, and I would like to believe it is only the fact that women are learning something new about their brothers. However, I suspect this may also be a more acceptable way for women to respond, as if they are taking care of men's feelings instead of touching and expressing their own anger.

It doesn't take much observation to notice how at the beginning of my workshops some males respond in a conditioned male manner. Their body language and verbal cues communicate the idea that this material is either nothing new or hardly worth considering. Some merely sit with arms folded across their chests, leaning way back in their chairs like distant and aloof observers, and some openly express that they expect little new or important from the workshop. Fortunately, I have asked these men just to hang on until the end, through my presentations and their processing. As a result, so many have expressed appreciation as they began to allow themselves to feel what it was like to grow up in a society with the gender conditioning we have begun to rehearse.

I'll never forget the one skeptical, male Christian minister, who began the workshop coolly, thoroughly disengaged and expecting little enlightenment. He even dismissed the ideas with, "I don't find anything new in this." At the end of the day he responded differently, "This is something we need to teach at least as early as high school. How can we get that done?"

FURTHER READING

Lois Gould, "X: A Fabulous Child's Story," in Amy Kesselman, Lily D. McNair, and Nancy Schniedewind, *Women: Images and Reality: A Multicultural Anthology.* Mountain View, CA: Mayfield, Publishing, 1995.

Harriet Goldhor Lerner, *The Dance of Anger: A Woman's Guide to Changing the Patterns of Intimate Relationships.* New York: Perennial, 1985.

William S. Pollack, *Real Boys: Rescuing Our Sons from the Myths of Manhood.* New York: Random House, 1998.

Deborah Tannen, *Talking from 9 to 5: Women and Men in the Workplace: Language, Sex, and Power.* New York: Avon Books, 1995.

Chapter Four

Boys Are Best and Some Are Even Better

There is no "separate but equal" in matters of gender either. The conditioning we experience growing up in the United States does more than convince us that the human qualities we all possess should be separated into two distinct genders, masculine and feminine. It does more than enforce the qualities it defines as "masculine" on boys while punishing boys who display other qualities. It does even more than enforce the qualities denied to boys on girls while punishing girls for displaying qualities it defines as masculine. Our social institutions also work together to install another conviction: that of the two genders society has defined for us, the masculine one is better.

When the system installs "masculinity" as one of two exclusive options, it doesn't teach us that the two options are equal. We are taught to believe that conditioned masculinity is the standard by which we measure everything. We are accustomed to our laws, texts, and statutes referring to all human beings as "he," "man," and "mankind." We often think of "man" as the human standard so that men regularly speak of their understandings of humanity as "human" while women speak of theirs as "a woman's perspective."

It is "masculine" traits that rule when we talk about how our nation should respond to other nations. An Iraqi president who acts out of his own culture's male gender conditioning, offends America. So, to restore American honor, we seem compelled to respond in a conditioned "manly" fashion to his "insult," as if he offended our nation's manliness. We are afraid that the world will take advantage of us if we look weak and unmanly.

In our national culture, "masculine" traits define our ideal of leadership. "Masculinity" is in charge of our public life. Our institutions, from the military, to government, to corporate boardrooms, are identified with conditioned masculinity. Women who would be leaders know better than to challenge it. In order to be elected, nominated, or promoted, they have to accept the value of "masculinity" and try to prove that they are even more "manly," or "just as good as a man."

Often we hear voices actually blaming "femininity," claiming that it is the cause of America's problems. Movements struggling for women's equality have been blamed for the failure of the family, the downsizing of workers, the corruption of American civilization, and the rise in immorality. A *Wall Street Journal* columnist responded to the hotly contested presidential election of 2000 by bemoaning the fact that American voters were so divided and blaming it on the "feminization" of American politics.

We defend "masculinity" more vigorously. We are more serious about offenses to "masculinity" and likely to judge more harshly those men who step out of the male role than women who portray "masculine" traits. Even our social initiatives are framed in terms of activities considered male. They are called "wars" and their leaders are often called "czars" — the war on poverty, the war on drugs, the war on illiteracy, the war on crime. And from Supreme Court justices and political leaders, we hear the battle cry of "Culture Wars" to respond to pro-gay activism. Seldom do we hear words like "nurturing" and "healing" in the publicity that promotes these efforts. And no matter how public rhetoric speaks of "motherhood" as honorable and important, "mothering" is another word not found in the discussion of social, political, and economic solutions.

It's Bad to Be Non-male

Since the better of the genders is the conditioned male, then it is worse to be defined as "non-male." One form of "non-male" is the feminine gender role women are conditioned to adopt and display. A girl learns the role and its lower status from birth because enforcement of the preference for the conditioned "male" begins in our earliest childhood interactions.

Even before they enter elementary school, boys learn male is better with taunts from other boys such as:

- You look like a girl.
- You act like a girl.
- You sound like a girl.
- You play girls' games.
- You throw a ball like a girl.
- You carry your books like a girl.
- You have a name that sounds like a girl's name.
- You walk like a girl.
- You run like a girl.

Little boys quickly internalize that the worst thing a boy can be is a girl and the best thing is a "real" (a masculine) boy. As early as four, studies show, boys are not only aware of masculine stereotypes, but they already know the value of working to live in terms of the preferred masculine role, and have begun to do so. As one researcher said of his four and five year olds: "We gave boys dolls and they used them as guns."

Through the conditioning reflected in these taunts, they also learn that a real boy is diametrically the opposite of a girl. In adult language, older boys and men will be criticized for acting "effeminate," for exhibiting those traits society reserves for women.

So conditioned masculinity will be at risk for the remainder of a man's life. The masculine role comes with the almost universal male fears that really he is not "man enough" and that this fact might be showing. Whenever his masculinity is questioned or threatened, he must react with conditioned male responses to fear and hurt, those emotions men are not supposed to have. Often he will display anger and the aggression that follows it toward the actual or perceived threat.

An elementary school boy already knows that when he is provoked, knocked down, or hit, he must come back fighting, not crying. To recover from the shame of the initial threat to his manhood, he feels it is necessary to display an even more "manly" reaction than the one that threatened him. That's because when shame is felt, honor must be won back through an exaggerated reaction which then threatens the other man even more intensely. So manhood next responds to the response with an even more exaggerated reaction. The violence escalates until the manliest one is proven.

A Girl's Role as a Lesser Being

A girl also learns that the worse thing she can be is who the culture is training her to be. And that is also who the culture is convincing her she naturally is — the conditioned definition of a girl.

This puts her in a double bind. First, her full humanity is subordinated to a limited gender role. Second, she, defined now by this limited feminine role, is subordinated to the masculine role. The qualities enforced on her to distinguish her from boys are devalued just as the qualities enforced on boys are praised.

A woman will be "put on a pedestal" only for embodying this inferior role. So, it is the role that is admired on that pedestal and the woman only when she embodies it well. She is to be the soft, gentle, nurturing "heart" of the home, while the man is the "head," leading as a real man does, with his brain and brawn. Some may pronounce these roles equal, but they will not declare women equal if they choose to live in all their humanity outside the role.

I often think about how much this may have changed until my undergraduate students tell me that they too remember when young boys considered girls cooties, scum, or contagious diseases. Being too close to a girl was considered dangerous, as if some contagion could infect and pollute a pristine masculinity.

Girls often internalized this and buried these evaluations so deeply that some now deny that the putdowns ever existed. The painful feelings linger beneath the surface, buried but not dead, to emerge in fear of success, or guilt when she does express power, independence, or self-affirmation. I remember one woman telling me that she loved competitive games and the quest to beat men and other women. She added, however, that when she did win, she felt guilty.

Women may internalize this evaluation as feelings of inferiority about the female body, female looks, female bodily cycles, and female intelligence. After all, they are expected to be physically weaker, and they are told they are attractive only for that brief period in which they embody the ideal of a youthful virgin. They are put down as subject to the control of natural forces they have difficulty conquering (note the jokes and other references to PMS), and considered intellectually less competent than men. In the past, even brain "size" comparisons were used by science to prove female inferiority, as if males use all of the brain they might possess, and without taking into account how brain dimensions related in both sexes to overall body size.

Women will subordinate their goodness, beauty, physical abilities, and experiences and replace them with feelings of inadequacy. Since they are supposed to be passive and dependent like children, when women do behave like independent adults they may not only be criticized by others but hear internal voices which will settle only for dependence again. They may take their lack of presence in upper-level positions in our major institutions as further proof of their inferior abilities. Such an internalized evaluation focuses the problem on them as women, not on the system.

Cultural observers call this internalized sexism. When women internalize these inferior valuations of their "femininity," they compensate by placing more value on the need to live the conditioned feminine role and on seeking male approval. If "real males" embody the accepted standard, the approval of well-conditioned males validates women for "doing the best women can," given their inferior status.

Some girls may fight against this lower evaluation with, "I'm just as good as a boy." Yet, this need to prove worth by the male standard still arises out of the persistence of the entrenched dominant evaluation. A girl's energy can be drained when she constantly fights this battle instead of freely creating her own life on her own terms and for her. She tries to "break the rules" in her fight against the lesser evaluation, but that is exactly the point. She is not challenging the rules themselves, merely evaluating herself against them. The more belligerent her response, the more she is focused on the superiority of masculinity.

As a few good friends and I sat in a small pizza restaurant one lazy winter afternoon, we listened to the friendly, out-going owner describe his athletic, college-age daughter. She was, without a doubt, a talented soccer player. We could recognize her abilities and talents even if we looked past the fact that these were the expressions of a proud father. She could be a star on any team. After recounting her crucial role in a recent match, he came to his final evaluation: "She's as good as any boy." For him, as for most of our culture, that was the measure of what was really "good." In the middle of the conditioning, it was a high complement.

Even in the days of women's success on athletic fields, the examples of runner Jackie Joyner Kersee and the U.S. Women's Soccer Team seem to function only as tokens in "women's" competition. Societies often allow a small number of any non-dominant group to reach a place near the top of some institutional ladders. The system displays these "tokens" to deny any cultural prejudices and to prove that the culture rewards people only on their merit. The few who make it are, therefore, very important to the system's view of reality. They allow a system's defenders to shift responsibility for the disparities between large groups of people away from the nature of the system itself. They place the blame for the vast majority who do not achieve such status onto the shoulders of the majority of individuals in the non-dominant group. It's their lack of personal ability, talents, or drive, not any institutionalized prejudices, that is the reason they too aren't successful.

Women who do succeed somewhat in this male culture are often "excused" for doing so. Their extraordinary efforts may be explained away as attempts to compensate for their lesser abilities, not for the greater energy it took to overcome their lower evaluation and the system's greater hurdles for women. That would be to admit the system's prejudices. Once successful, though, women may be ignored, "seen [even displayed] but not heard."

By internalizing the inferior evaluation of the "feminine," other women may view women who succeed as too much — too masculine, too aggressive, too manipulative, too "brainy," too controlling, too domineering, or just too "different." Women who move into positions of authority often find themselves isolated from the majority of women, and even lose some of their female friends, who don't feel they measure up to the successful woman's unusual abilities. In addition, successful women themselves often report feeling guilty in the midst of their own success. They suspect that the reason they are still not being taken seriously by their male colleagues is something they are not doing right. There must be something innately inferior about them or their backgrounds.

Girls are conditioned to accept this inferior evaluation from the culture. They come to believe it through the elementary years and many seek to live it out well. Living this devalued role has its rewards because the alternative is even further victimization. Their choice is no more free than that given boys. They must live in terms of the least awful alternative. Further victimization means they too will receive violence and its threats, ridicule, and rejection from boys, girls, and adults who are accustomed to evaluating themselves in terms of the systemic conditioning. To compensate for accepting the role, a girl may have to convince herself of its value by doing all she can to exalt the "feminine" and to accept her dependence on male evaluations of her being. She will later come to believe that her connections with men are what validate her.

BEAT OR BE BEATEN, THE WORLD OF BOYS

This dynamic teaches young boys that "real" boys, and later "real" men devalue girls. Boys learn to praise and reward "masculine" qualities, responses, and attitudes they are conditioned to manifest and to envy the boy who represents this "masculinity" the best. They put girls down through shaming, disgracing, and mocking them just because they are girls.

One of the recurring themes in the popular, late twentieth-century, comic strip "Calvin and Hobbs" shows young Calvin expressing his contempt for girls, especially when he hangs out alone with his stuffed tiger Hobbs in a club house with a sign that reads: "No girls allowed." Girls are treated as the worst things both by glorification of the ideal "boy" and by direct criticism of what is "feminine." Boys are conditioned to accept each other to the extent that they join in the demeaning of girls.

In terms of the categories used to analyze oppression of various forms, the earliest relationship of boys to girls is the classic relationship of an "oppressor" group to a "victim" group. As individuals, boys and girls are not inherently either one, of course. Oppression is a systemically conditioned group to group relationship. In response to it, individual boys and girls, and later men and women, will almost automatically, even without thinking, negotiate their individual relationships.

The alternative to identifying with these roles is to choose to step out of the roles and face society's sanctions for doing so. Boys would not accept a role that mistreats girls and views them as inferior without the fear-based conditioning that alters their view of reality — in fact they would do everything in their power to stop any mistreatment. Girls would not work to be the best victim of this role if they were allowed to maintain contact with their full, inborn humanity. But the result of the conditioning is to set boys up as a group in a place of power and dominance over girls who are set up to be victims of that dominance. All individuals have been hurt by our culture, and the conditioning hurts both boys and girls, but the result of the conditioning which hurts and limits boys is that they are taught to fulfill an oppressor role.

This boy-girl relationship will continue and intensify throughout the elementary school years and soon be taken for granted. Our institutions, including the psychology that supports the system, will even treat this dynamic as "natural." In a 1999 U.S. Supreme Court decision, *Davis v. Monroe County Board of Education,* the Court was asked to decide a case of sexual harassment by an elementary school boy toward a girl. The justices on both sides of the decision assumed throughout that this relationship of oppressor to victim is quite normal, even natural, for young children. In their written opinions, they blamed it on student immaturity or "childish misconduct" rather than on this early conditioning, and were able to effortlessly list insults, banter, teasing, name-calling, shoving, pushing, and gender specific conduct as examples of this "normal" behavior. A large percentage of our school age children, the court said matter-of-factly, will experience something they consider sexual harassment. The highest court in the land was saying: "that's just the way things are."

The relationship of boys to boys is also dominated by this conditioning. Male-male relationships become more like the relationships of one oppressor to another. Boys learn that the open expression of emotions — the way girls are supposed to do naturally — will bring the same consequences from other boys that girls receive much of the time, from violence, to ridicule, to isolation. Generally these responses will come from boys, but parents and other adults will reinforce them. Boys learn that the masculine world is a dangerous place to express emotions or any other vulnerability.

Fear of dependency, vulnerability, and weakness, enforces the need to appear tough and to develop emotional, psychological, and physical armor. As one teenage boy said to me as I read a portion of this chapter to him, if you show vulnerability "other boys will eat you up."

"Beefing up" is not just a body-building activity for males. As one man expressed his own approach: "Whenever I first meet another man, I size him up and compare myself to him. I'm really trying to determine if I can beat him." The most common world for the young boy is just that, a "beat or be beaten" world.

By the time they enter kindergarten, and for some even earlier, boys begin to reject any public display of affection from their parents. The parental touch that we know was crucial to the very life of the child and which they took for granted and cherished earlier, boys now must reject in public. It is now necessary for them to bury their feelings behind "big boy" expectations. Many parents remember when their sons told them not to kiss them goodbye or give them a public hug because such a display would bring criticism from other boys. Looking too close, even to their parents, would not fit the isolation real boys should become accustomed to displaying, but be ridiculed, humiliated, and even rejected.

Boys' games become increasingly competitive to enforce the emotional distance that is necessary between oppressors. Even before competition is fully enforced through "organized" sports — that is athletic competitions defined in adult terms by and for adults, this mark of masculinity is installed. Winning has its rewards.

Competition with other boys leads to defining most male-male relationships as competitive. Boys learn they can only win at the expense of other boys. Losers are often ridiculed. Those men who finish second in world sporting events such as the Olympics, are seldom remembered. They are often personally haunted by the shame of losing instead of the pride that comes from being the second best on the entire planet. Even the words "second best," sound like failure to men in this competitive world view. Men are taught that every success they have in life is at someone else's expense, particularly other males. Competing with girls is less noble than beating another male. Young, and not so young, boys, will shame another for "beating a girl." Clearly this is an inferior, even "unmanly" act. Real boys beat other boys; they win when other boys lose.

As this further separates male from male, oppressor from oppressor, it functions to maintain the total system. An important prerequisite for the system's own success is the sacrifice of human closeness. The fear of that closeness, homophobia, enforces the oppressor-oppressor dynamic. If I get too close to another man, I might relate to him as a fellow human being, who feels and loves. That would make it harder to do anything that is at his expense. Victories where someone else pays an emotional, economic, physical, or other price so that I can win will be harder to justify, value, and savor.

Men need to fear closeness to keep this oppressor-oppressor dynamic and its competitive system going. The systemic view of reality values these competitive relationships because they prepare boys to be the "real men" who are successful in our military and economic systems. These men are truly competent and virile. They even look as if they have "beaten the odds." Actually, they have beaten other men. They are unmoved by the price these losers paid and unaware of the sacrifice of their humanity they had to make in order to win. Male "team work" after all, is often the ability of one group of men to work together to beat, defeat, or kill another group of men. Any men who hesitate should "suck it up," "grow up," "take it like a man,"or "get over it."

Boys who do not find an area of life where they can defeat other boys, feel shamed. The best boys find that area of competency the earliest, and "stick to it." However, even those who win, ultimately come up against someone who is better. They remain unsatisfied.

Yet, their disappointment and dissatisfaction seldom prompts attitudinal changes regarding the conditioned male need to compete. Instead it often results in male disappointment, bitterness, feelings of inadequacy, failure, impotency, suicide, the blaming and scapegoating of others, and/or a search for new arenas for success, such as right-wing militia organizations. Masculinity is so entrenched that few men are ready to challenge the conditioned masculine gender role itself.

Girls may join the criticism of boys who do not put down girls the way boys should, but boys are far more often the ones who punish other boys until they join them in the demeaning of girls. If a boy tells his fellows that he likes girls or thinks that girls are as good as boys, if he tells them that girls' games are just as fun as boys' games, if he should admire any "feminine" qualities, if he refuses to play competitively or boisterously enough, and has close female friends, he will be treated as a "girly boy," a "wuss," a "pussy," a "sissy," "a Sally." He will be victimized. Even his parents and his friends' parents might wonder about him.

A Boy's Uneasy Alternatives

This leaves a boy with two uneasy alternatives. He will feel as if he must face them alone, isolated, and without any allies, because the other boys cannot talk about these issues in terms of how they really feel. And few adult males want to relive those emotions by sharing them with a young boy. A boy can join the other boys in treating girls as lesser beings, or he can become a victim of the other boys. He will be put down until he joins the putting down, victimized until he accepts the oppressor role. Sometimes the best he will be able to do is to remain silent and collude with the demeaning of girls. He will be fully accepted, even admired, though when he participates openly with the other boys in enforcing the role on each other.

By the time they have entered kindergarten, boys know that there is an even more effective and despised putdown that will keep them in their learned male role as oppressor. A number of studies of early elementary school students have shown that the two worse names children can be called are "dumb" and "queer." For most early elementary students "queer," "fag," and "gay" are considered bad without an understanding of their full content. Yet, what children do know is that being called these "names" means a child is not acting the way a boy or a girl should. They know it has to do with their gender role. "That's so gay," becomes a put down for any unacceptable activity. And it won't be long before boys play a game called "Smear the Queer."

I was confronted with this early use of labels such as "gay, queer, and fag" as general putdowns by four and five year old boys one day as I stood talking with my neighbor on her front lawn. Her young boys were playing with the neighbor boys when we were both startled by one neighbor boy calling those he didn't like "butt-fuckers." We asked him if he knew what this meant. He didn't, but he knew it was bad. He had obviously heard this somewhere in our middle-class neighborhood and not from adults talking about an act practiced by some heterosexual couples. Some sexologists estimate that well over twenty percent practice this form of intimate activity. In any case, I more fully realized what studies of early elementary school children are showing, that children use the language of "gay," "queer," and "fag," more than many suspect. In my workshops since I have listened to parents of young children tell of their own shock when they heard children use these as putdowns of other children.

I attended a 1999 screening for community leaders of the film *It's Elementary: Talking About Gay Issues in School.* A Kansas City public television station arranged the gathering to prepare the community for the film's controversial broadcast. What surprised these leaders most was that even the youngest elementary school children shown in the film already knew about "homosexuals." Contrary to the protests the station received from people who had not seen the film and who wrote that showing it would expose children too early to the concept of homosexuality, these early elementary school children had already formed opinions about the topic. And their most memorable source of information about its meaning was the negative stereotypes found in the media. One example familiar to most of the children was a scene in the film *Ace Ventura: Pet Detective.* The hero, played by Jim Carey, had just realized that he had kissed another man. The "humor" that followed showed him using every means to purge himself of the resulting pollution, even using a plunger on his mouth to induce vomiting. Children had already been exposed to the images, and they pictured "gay" as dirty and unnatural and at times evidenced by two men kissing, even though this is commanded in the Bible and the norm in much of Europe.

What happens, then, at this early period to boys who

refuse to treat girls as inferiors, who refuse to demean them and affirm their inferiority in this manner, who refuse to participate in an oppressor role toward girls or other boys? These boys are put down as "queer" and "fag," and will receive the sanctions of the conditioning to attempt to force them back into the mainstream. These general putdowns punish them as early as ages four or five for not acting in terms of the male gender role. Real males demean girls. "Queer" and "fag" are used to ridicule these boys for not really appearing masculine.

In a culture where the conditioned male is best, there is a second form of non-male: the male who does not live the conditioned role of oppressor and may not evidence enough homophobia. Some males, then, are really men, and some are not. If boys do not live as conditioned males, they will be put down as non-males. They will receive the same treatment as girls. One teenage boy described the feeling of this demeaning to me: "It can feel like death."

This is the first stage of installing gay oppression. The oppression of gay men has nothing to do with who is having sex with whom or who is in love with whom. In fact, it has nothing to do with sexual orientation or homosexuality at all. It is a means of installing and enforcing a conditioned gender role. It teaches men through fear of the consequences how society says they must relate to others. Real men are supposed to relate to women in classic oppressor-victim terms and to each other in classic oppressor-oppressor terms. Gay oppression begins as a subset of sexism. Real men should not relate to each other in any manner other than oppressor to oppressor. They should certainly not get close in any human way. If they get too close or they step out of the masculine role, they will be victimized by other men. If they feel threatened by other men, they will have to react as "real men" are taught to react to fear, or be victimized.

As a boy enters elementary school in our dominant culture, he has a choice. He can either join mainstream male conditioning and participate in demeaning girls and enforcing the oppressor role on other boys, or he will be treated as a "queer," with violence, threats, ridicule, and rejection by his fellow boys.

It's important to notice that this is not a boy's free choice or a choice made out of a boy's connection with his complete, inborn humanity. The choice is made out of terror during what some researchers therefore call the first crisis point in a boy's life, ages four to six. He makes this choice not in order to live freely or to flourish in life, but to survive in our system of conditioning. He chooses it as a way out of victimization, out of a victim role. It is the least awful alternative available to the young boy. The way out of victimization is to live and cherish "manhood" defined as an oppressor role. In this role he is assured acceptance through participating in demeaning other boys who slip, who don't display manhood well, or who refuse to demean girls. And they are the "fags" and the "queers."

A GIRL'S ALTERNATIVES AS VICTIM

The system defines a girl's role as one of a victim. By definition, a victim depends on others for validation, for the correct interpretation of her experiences, for praise, for her happiness, and, often, for her survival itself, particularly on those in the oppressor role. A "real" girl is supposed to be demeaned and devalued, put down by boys in terms of the superiority of conditioned "masculinity." Her job is to work to be the girl who fulfills the victim role the best. She is to learn to value the victim role, believe it is not victimization, believe it is natural, and help enforce this role on other girls. She may even join men who use the diminutive term "girls" to refer to grown women or put down "women drivers" or the "catty" women at the office.

The conditioning defines her relationships to other girls in victim-victim terms. As such, she will compete with other girls to be the "best" victim rather than fighting to end the role itself. So, the victim role has girls vying with each other for male attention and approval, working in competition with other girls to be the best example of male concepts of female beauty, subordinating their needs to those of men, defining their "feminine" success in how well they get male attention, and deferring their intelligence, strength and power to that of males.

A girl may assume the inevitability of the victimization as well as the role, feel comfortable in its familiarity, and look for "advantages" within the role. That a woman would settle for the symbolism of the "chivalry"of a man who opens a door for her rather than the reality of equal pay for equal work, is the victim role. She will value other women to the extent that they live the role. To do otherwise would be to question the very role she has put much effort into living. She might make excuses for women's lesser advancement in comparison to male achievements by referring to women's lesser abilities or deficient backgrounds, or just with, "that's the way women are."

Girls may eventually seek out males for approval who cannot give that approval to them. They might reject the "nice guy" in order to win the guy who isn't so nice. One young woman explained why she had always been attracted to men who demeaned women this way: "I want to be treated nicely by guys whose only reason to be nice would be that they were compelled to change by their love for me as their special girl." Romance novels which are popular reading for women often feature a hero who is unlikely to commit to or care about women until he is changed by an overwhelming love for the heroine. That is real proof that she is loveable and the best "girl" of all. As the heroine in the 1998 movie *Titanic* remembered her rogue hero, "He saved me in every way a woman can be saved. . . ."

What happens to the girl in early elementary school who fights against this early demeaning? She is the one who refuses to lose in "boys' games" or refuses to take the putdowns of her male peers. She doesn't "fix herself up" or "act like a lady."

She may even fight back physically. She decides what is important to her, excels at typically "masculine" mechanical and gross motor tasks, and values her body for how it functions to enable and empower her.

She will be put down by men and other women not only for stepping out of the role, but for any successes she has at the achievements which should affirm men's "manhood." Women who live the "masculine" role threaten conditioned males. Men may fear these women are "more manly" than males believe themselves to be. That in itself raises the system's anxiety. "She's more of a man than you are." "She wears the pants in your family." Violence, threats of violence and ridicule are sure to follow to protect "masculinity." And women who identify with the victim role will join in the putdowns, though usually less violently.

Because the superiority of the conditioned male role in our culture conditions us to take "femininity" less seriously than "masculinity," the "non-female" actions of a young girl may be considered "cute," "harmless," or insignificant while she is young. She may be called a "tomboy," not an example of the feminine ideal, not a "real girl." Society will tolerate her female deviation for a number of years while the media bombards her with images of real women. She may find girls who join with her in rejection of the victim role, though the girls at school who receive the most positive attention will conform. At some point, though, her mother may take her aside and advise her that she will not "attract men" as long as she challenges the role. She will end up an "old maid" or a "spinster" and be suspected of something even worse.

If she bonds too closely with her female friends without concern for male evaluation, she will hear the words "lesbian" and "dyke" as further putdowns. Conditioned girls are supposed to be competing with each other to be victims, not getting close as human beings.

A mother came up to me after one of my workshops to tell

me about her daughter's experience in preschool. One day after school, her daughter asked, "Mom, what's a lesbo?" Her mother's questions discovered that her preschool daughter had been holding hands with her best female friend at recess. She had been picked on by both boys and girls on the playground, who introduced her to the label without knowing its meaning. They did know however that, whatever it meant, it was bad. Could she ever hold hands with another girl again? In preschool she was learning not to get that close to someone of the same sex.

At this early age, then, children show the first stage of the oppression of lesbians. Just as it was for the first stage of gay male oppression, the oppression of lesbians has nothing to do with sex, sexual orientation, or who is in love with whom. It is the means of installing and enforcing a gender role on women, a role that is intended to keep women apart, a homophobia. "Lesbian" and "dyke" as general putdowns will eventually be attached to lesbians in our culture.

The conditioning says that girls are not supposed to be oppressors. Unless they submit to the victim role, they will be victimized further. That further victimization is being treated as a non-female female, a female who does not live the gender role, a lesbian. This choice of living the victim role or further victimization is not a free one for the young girl. Its motivation is survival in a system that is homophobic. Which is the least awful alternative for the elementary school girl?

Learning We Are "Opposite" Sexes

As children proceed through elementary school, they continue to learn the gender roles. Though psychoanalysts may have labeled this period latency, as if little is happening, girls and boys are further subjected to the kind of information about each other which deepens the conditioning.

Boys and girls are divided from each other to do this. Sometimes institutions are created to separate them literally.

There are boys and girls clubs, boys and girls scouts, boys and girls classes, boys and girls lines, even boys and girls schools.

Observing children at about eight years old who have already been conditioned into oppressor and victim relationships, psychologists assure us that this polarization is "normal" and, maybe, "desirable." With "explanations" such as boys and girls want to play with children like themselves, or this split along gender lines is a "natural" part of childhood "and doesn't call for a great deal of parental concern," the dominant psychological community blesses this split as healthy.

In many of these assertions, one hears the results of the expert's own previous conditioning. One pediatrics professor explained, without batting an eye, that this split was okay because it was a means of reinforcing and internalizing the gender roles: "Boys are trying to identify themselves as boys, and girls are doing the same." Others agree and point out how the roles are enforced by members of a child's own sex, assuring parents that it is "normal" for children at this age to feel compelled to win the approval of same-sex peers, "who are often quick to ridicule any intermingling." It's just the way it is. But would it happen if it weren't for the earlier on-going gender conditioning which separates the genders?

Separating the sexes enables each sex to learn about the other without the interference of living examples who might object to what is being said about them. Girls learn who real girls are, and they learn what boys are like. Boys are taught who real boys are and what girls are like. The separation allows the system to pass on much misinformation.

When the sexes come together at puberty, the gender roles are thoroughly entrenched. Each thinks of the other not merely as a different sex but as members of "the opposite sex." Convinced that the conditioning is inherent, the sexes are now opposed to each other. No wonder the stories will fly about the inability of men to understand women and vice versa.

When my son was about two, I used to play "the opposite

game" with him. His eyes would light up with the delight children show when they know an answer to an adult's question. He proudly responded to "high" with "low," "big" with "little," and "short" with "long." I remember the day I added "boy" to the list and he responded "man." He had not yet been taught to think of girls as the opposite of him. Given a few more years of conditioning, he would.

By the time children have completed elementary school, they have been thoroughly conditioned into their gender roles. They have been taught how to relate as oppressors and victims, and they have been taught what will happen to them if they do not submit to the roles. The first stage of the oppression of gay men and lesbians has been installed to enforce the roles, and they have been taught by every institution around them that boys are best.

One adult male told me of the most effective means used by his elementary school teachers to punish boys. "If you don't straighten out," the boys were regularly told, "you will have to sit with the girls." It was a punishment and a lesson enforced by the adults around him. Their message to him was that to sit with a girl was the worst fate. If the girls also believed this message from the adult authorities in that school, they would have experienced a double bind. They could not sit with the boys, and they had to sit as the worst among the worst. Real boys were best. The children all knew non-males were worst.

FURTHER READING

"Oppression," in Marilyn Frye, *The Politics of Reality: Essays in Feminist Theory*. Trumansburg, NY: The Crossing Press, 1983.

Shere Hite, *The Hite Report on the Family: Growing Up Under Patriarchy*. New York: Grove Press, 1994.

CHAPTER FIVE

GETTING A MAN AND GETTING LAID

Of course, boys and girls aren't separated forever. Our cultural ideals see to that. But their separation ends only when the gender role software has been installed. It ends when appropriate oppressor and victim roles have been identified as the roles of "real" boys and "real" girls. It ends when they have been convinced by the system that these male and female roles are essential, inborn, and inherent.

The separation ends when girls and boys have learned to think of each other as not merely different but "opposite" (that is, opposed) sexes. "Opposite sex" closeness is now "appropriate." As "opposites" we guarantee misunderstanding and confusion between boys and girls when they come back together. They will connect under a different set of agreements than they would if they had been allowed to maintain their complete in-born similarities as human beings. By the time they show interest in each other, they believe that these opposing roles are who they are. Both boys and girls are now expected to develop relationships according to the "appropriate" patterns of male/female closeness defined by the system's conditioning.

When the sexes do come together again, it's that fascinating and confusing time called puberty. If the time is confusing, however, the gender roles seem clear. They provide what appear to be an unchanging set of standards that society can count on as the boy or girl navigates puberty.

It seems more likely that the apparent confusion of puberty is promoted, or at least exaggerated, by the demands of the roles themselves. The more tightly the "manhood" and "womanhood" roles are defined, the less boys and girls are allowed to live and grow flexibly and freely as human beings and the more they are afraid that they do not adequately fulfill their appropriate roles.

No matter how the roles may fail us all, we cling to them desperately in order to make it through what even our conditioned psychological professionals label a "natural" confusion of the teen years. We are taught to blame any problems we have with the roles not on them or the system but on the fact that we are not living them closely enough. "If I could only be more of a man, then I'd be okay." Or, "If I only didn't have such a misshapen body for a woman, then I'd be more attractive."

THE REAL WOMAN'S GOAL: GETTING A MAN

Along with the acceptance of the victim role that both defined feminine traits and convinced the young girl that somehow she is less than a boy, a girl has learned by junior high school that her most important life task is to set out to "get a man." She is taught this regardless of what her sexual orientation may be. In recent times she is often taught that there may be other things she can do along the way, even finish her education and develop a temporary career. However, at some point she is to seek the man who will provide her with the "real" fulfillment that the conditioning says a woman cannot provide for herself through her own means.

Popular literature, even when it speaks of female self-fulfillment, still begins with the assumption that a woman's life is incomplete without a male companion and the fulfillment of children she herself bears. Journalist Susan Faludi in *Backlash* has documented the media's inaccurate use of statistics to enforce women's fears that postponing their search for men by pursuing a career is likely to bring unhappiness and depression. From everywhere the message to women is clear: Don't wait. Don't put it off too long. You need the fulfillment only a husband and family can bring. All your independent pursuits are fleeting in comparison to "getting a man" and being a mother.

This suits the victim role imposed on women well, for if the system says women are almost nothing and men are the best, the only way to be something is to get one of those "worthwhile" things, a man. Generally, women are not taught the ultimate value of protecting themselves, standing on their own two feet, joining with others to provide equal pay for equal work so that financial dependence on men is unnecessary, and finding their worth in themselves and other women. The conditioning ultimately defines their "femininity" in terms of how successful they are at "getting a man."

The system teaches young girls that the reason they must "get a man" is to have someone who can, and will, "love and protect" them. In fact, a girl's worth, the system says, is found in her ability to get a man who appears able to love her, give her attention, take care of her, and protect her.

When I ask women what that man is supposed to protect them from, they usually answer, "other men." They realize, on the one hand, that men as a group are conditioned into the role of oppressors of women. As such, women are like those who are conditioned into the victim role in the dynamics of any oppression — they learn to fear the oppressor.

Men hold a similar fear of each other. They too fear other men as their potential oppressors, but they cannot admit to themselves, much less speak of, that emotion without feeling that they are unmanly or fearing that they will receive further victimization.

The problem is that on the other hand, a woman is supposed to be saved by one of those men, the one she is to "get," even though the conditioning has installed into women a deep fear of men as a group. Women are again put into a double bind. To make oneself vulnerable to men feels down right scary, and yet that is what the "real woman" is conditioned to do with the one "right" man. She desperately needs a "Mr. Right" to be different from all other men, and she hopes and convinces herself that he will be.

What women fear is not males as a sex but males thinking and acting as conditioned men. They fear the masculine role they expect men to act out. They fear masculinity's anger and its accompanying violence, its isolation, and its emptiness of emotional expression. They fear male strength turned into manhood posturing, masculine addictions, and conditioned manhood's patterns of relating.

Yet women are still convinced by the conditioning to hunt for the one man who is a member of this group of conditioned men to "protect" them. Somehow a man, they are taught, is the key to making it in the system. Women can't do it on their own, but the man can beat it. He can keep away the effects of the sexism and the victim role. He can show a woman that, in spite of the fact that as a female she is the worst, he, the best, not only accepts her but proves she is loveable by that acceptance. It may not matter whether he is a good man to others, even other girls. He can be ruthless to them, but if he loves her, it proves this girl is especially loveable.

Even conditioned images of the ideal man reflect this need. For most women, the ideal man for a life partner does not wear a skimpy thong that shows his body parts as he walks down a model's runway. He is usually older (which means more experienced), maybe with graying temples, and wears a business suit, the uniform of the man who has worked the system and succeeded in or over it. This is the man who best displays that he has the abilities and resources to protect his woman from the system. He has all the marks of one who has come out on top.

Some women might prefer a muscled man or the big man, under whom his woman will feel protected. That too is an image of the ability to protect a woman from harm. For men, too, muscles are an armor to protect them from other men. For the woman, in addition, his stature is a sign that he can keep away her fear of failing as a woman. She is a good enough woman to get one of those. Getting him is her sign of success.

The young girl might also be told that she needs a man in order to raise "his children." The conditioning that women need children in order to be fulfilled as women is particularly strong in most cultures. Though we know that nothing outside of oneself can provide real fulfillment, children are recommended to women as a way to "feel fulfilled as a woman." They are regularly brought into the world in order to do what children could never do — make adults feel fulfilled. As astute observers, children will learn that this is why they are here. They will feel the burden of fulfilling their parents' needs and be told by society that it is appropriate for them to bear the weight of their parents' need for fulfillment. Whether it is in the areas of sports, education, fame, finance, or a "better marriage," children often find themselves fulfilling their unfulfilled parents' dreams.

Women are still expected to be the primary child care providers in our society. When daycare is used as an option, women are the ones who are taught to bear the guilt for not taking sufficient time for, or interest in, their children. They are at times called "selfish" and not sufficiently committed to their children. When there are a few discussions of the problems of a working dad in our society, these pale in comparison to the regularity of discussions of the problems of the working mom. She, not he, is the one who must "choose" between work and family, and she will be blamed for not raising "his" or "their" children. Girls learn this fact early as they hunt for that man whose children they will raise. They are learning that the role of the ideal mother is one of many self-sacrifices. That self-sacrificing mother who gave up so much for her husband and children and the "woman behind the man" are images still highly praised by the system.

Now, anyone in the victim role of oppression, whether it be racism, sexism or heterosexism, knows they must carefully learn about the oppressor in order to survive. A false move or a mistake due to insufficient knowledge of the actions and characteristics of the dominant group can be devastating, resulting in threats, ridicule, and rejection by the group who is supposed to validate the victim. Since the protection of a victimized group is based on that group staying in the victim role, even members of the victimized group will react negatively to the misstep of one of its own because that misstep calls attention to the group in ways which call forth further victimization.

So women must know men's conditioned role more thoroughly than men need to know about women's role. The most popular women's magazines are filled with articles about understanding "your man," pleasing "your man," helping "your man," and fitting your lives and needs in with "your man's needs." Men's magazines seldom broach the subject except to encourage men to play their dominant role more effectively through being better at control, power, financial success, and sex.

The competition for "Mr. Right" further separates girls who before puberty had found their meaning and safety in each other. It contributes to the homophobia in women who compete to live the role of the best victim, the one most attractive to men. Girls might actually compete openly for the same boy. They might compete merely in fantasizing about the same boy and what it would be like if he "picked me." On the one hand, feeling that she, unlike all the other girls, is special to him because she has been chosen by a man means she has won a competition with other girls for a man. This competition and "victory" separate her from all those others of her sex and thereby promote same-sex distance and isolation. On the other hand, many girls will separate from the one who is successful at attracting male attention, feeling they are just not as good, pretty, sexy, or talented as the cheerleader and homecoming queen. Women often speak of the isolation from other women they experience when they appear to be successfully living the role.

The conditioning also convinces women about how best to "get a man." They learn that they will not get one through their intelligence, power, leadership, courage, alliance with all women, feminism, strength, or competency. They are not going to get a man through their athletic ability, especially if they are able to compete successfully with him or beat him every time they go bowling or play tennis. They must lose at sports they play with men if they are interested in them. He can then fulfill his male role by "showing her" how to do it better.

So, women learn to demur, to lose or to feign losing, a pattern that, if internalized, will guarantee women will express lesser abilities in athletic and other contests. Girls who before had shown their strength, talents, and intellect, soon learn to downplay them.

Researchers identify early adolescence as the first crisis point for girls. It's when they most devalue and suppress their emotions, blunt their insights, and step back from many previous achievements which threaten men. Adolescent girls discover, as psychologist Mary Pipher has carefully described it in her book *Reviving Ophelia,* that they cannot be both "feminine" and "adult." They are to take on the characteristics of children rather than adult human beings. Whereas adults are to be active, independent, and logical, girls are to be passive, dependent and illogical. Studies show that in early adolescence girls' IQ, math, and science scores drop; they are less optimistic, assertive, energetic, resilient, curious, or inclined to take risks, while they become more self-critical, depressed and deferential. The conditioning has convinced them these changes are necessary to be successful at their main life task — getting a man.

Women are taught that to get a man they will need to look weak, delicate, dainty, petite, demure, needy, and not too bright, particularly when it comes to practical tasks like auto mechanics at which real men are supposed to succeed. "Dumb blond jokes" epitomize and enforce this image. "Blondes have more fun," it has been said. That was because they were the best models of male-defined femininity, and many women bought into to this by mimicking that image through the variety of "beauty" products offered by modern chemistry. Young girls learn from parents, teachers, and peers that they must look like they need protection to "get a man."

This need to look weak and helpless at "important" tasks, in turn supports the male conditioning which says that manhood depends upon the ability of real men to protect their women and that women inherently need male protection. In war, one of the conditioned male acts which puts down other men is to rape the women of the enemy. This proves that their enemies have failed as men because they were unable to protect "their" women. Rape, as many writers have pointed out, is not an act of male sexual relief but an act of male dominance. It not only asserts dominance over women, but over the men who have failed to do what real men do: protect "their" women. Male rage at other men's violence directed against women, can often be an anger that covers the fear that these men have failed as men to protect "their" women: mothers, daughters, sisters, wives, and the women of their tribe, clan, religious community, or country.

What girls have learned by early puberty about the key to "getting a man" for love and protection is that their looks, their body and body parts, and sex are what does it. They think less of how their bodies function for themselves to accomplish their goals and more about its form and how it appears to others. Few girls feel they meet up to the concept of beauty demanded by the "best" men, but the image of female beauty and its accompanying body parts has been thoroughly internalized by most junior high girls and explains the increasing rate of teen plastic surgery. Barbie dolls, adult women around them, even female heroes who are strong warriors, display this image of beauty.

The media tell girls that if they do not have this image "naturally," they are fortunate enough to be able to buy beauty. Few girls do match the ideal as culture portrays it. Thus, the economic system thrives on the image of the "successful" girl who is beautiful enough to "get a man."

The system also sets a girl up in the victim role in terms of the system's conditioning about sex. She must use sex to "get a man" but she must not do so aggressively. There are names for aggressive girls and they are not like those given to "experienced" boys. They are "sluts" "bitches" and "whores" in terms of moral judgements, or "nymphomaniacs" in terms of psychological putdowns. None of these would be the girls who "get a man" to love and protect them.

Add to this the Western romantic tradition reflected in films, books, music, and television and the victim role is reinforced. If a girl accepts this version of "romance" as the truth about how she will find the man who will save her from the further victimization surrounding "spinsterhood," she will also feel uniquely fortunate to have actually gotten one. Success, according to this mythology, is quite iffy:

- If she is pretty enough and her make-up is just right.
- If she is in the right place at the right time and doesn't miss one of her few chances.
- If she says the right things.
- If the stars and moon are right.

- If she is dressed just right.
- If she flashes her perfectly made up eyes just right and smiles just right.
- If she dances, walks, and stands just right.
- If she isn't too forward but flirts just right.
- If she responds to his advances just right.
- If she doesn't overdo anything.

Then, maybe, just maybe, the mythology says, she will "get a man." She will be able to sing: "I was half; now I'm whole." Living as half a person will have "paid off" and finally she will be "complete." Such is the victim role defined for the teenage girl in junior high and high school.

What happens to her when the attitude of the man that she has "gotten" seems to get worse than the sexism "out there"? That will depend on how much she can still muster her own inborn self-acceptance and abilities, those that the conditioning denied her. She may be able to leave that man, or she may use all of the excuses that women use to stay with a man even if he is abusive:

- He doesn't mean it, really.
- He really does love me.
- He has his problems too.
- He said he was sorry and would be better.
- I can change things if I just try harder.
- I can't make it on my own.
- I have nowhere else to go or no one else to turn to.
- There's no one better out there.
- He really needs me.

If she does leave, she will have to face the feelings of being a "failed" woman. She will fear becoming "an old maid," a "spinster," or she may be called even worse, unless she does not wait too long to begin her search for another man to fulfill her. She will do all of this is in order to live a gender role that has put her out of touch with her complete humanity. That gender role conditions girls and women to respond to the conditioning being installed in boys.

A Real Man's Goal: Getting Laid

When boys enter puberty, they too have been thoroughly taught that "real men" seek to "get a woman." They are taught this no matter what their sexual orientation. Though they may be unclear or confused about their erotic preference, given that all the pressure is to be heterosexual, this one thing is clear. They must "get a woman" as proof that they are real men. If they are unable to do this, they are deficient as males.

Notice, however, that in junior high and high school, the images presented to boys about "getting a woman," are dramatically different from those taught to girls about "getting a man." Whereas the ideals of mother, sacrificer, homemaker, and wife dominate the conditioning regarding female fulfillment, the male ideal is found in men like Special Agent 007, the football hero, the handsome, detached rogue, the carefree adventurer, or the warrior fully committed to little but his fight to defeat other men. What these men have in common besides their devil-may-care attitude toward danger or their own demise is they can "get" any woman they want into bed.

For the boy entering puberty, the image of the "real man" who "gets a woman," is not a commitment to closeness and intimacy with a female human being. "Getting a woman" in junior high and high school means "getting laid."

We need to remember that "getting laid" is really gender conditioning for boys. The system teaches us that somehow "getting laid," as with all its gender conditioning, is "natural." It is also supposed to be "just the way things are." The system teaches us to justify and excuse this conditioned role as another element of the claim that "boys will be boys."

Since "getting laid" is male gender role conditioning, it has nothing to do with inborn human sexuality, with sex, or with the male sex drive. Its conditions are internalized through the means by which the system installs all conditioning, summed up as fear and even terror. Thus, this conditioning is marked by dysfunction, for it puts males out of touch with who they really are and what their sexuality might really be. "Getting laid" is so internalized by both men and women that it is thought of as sex and labeled the male sex drive. Both men and women are convinced of it.

One of the clearest delineations that summarizes the dynamics of "getting laid" which are studied by researchers, is the outline used by men's workshop leader Charlie Kreiner. In workshops across the country, he condenses the research in terms of nine "layers" or characteristics. Let me expand on them.

Understanding each of these layers is crucial to understanding the confusion that exists regarding sex and sexuality in our culture. Each layer confuses both men and women because, like all male-based conditioning in cultures where "boys are best," women's conditioning sets women up to respond to all the layers of male conditioning.

Without the systemic conditioning of women, these layers of male conditioning would not work at all. Studies of magazines aimed at or read by teenage women in the 1990's, such as *YM, Teen, Seventeen, Glamour,* and *Mademoiselle,* conclude that these magazines explain to young women that they should define sex in terms of the desires of men, and that a woman's sexuality is meant to accommodate men. When researchers compared these magazines to the advice given in marriage and home economics manuals published earlier in the twentieth century, they found that both groups advised women to determine what a man wants and to concentrate on pleasing him. The difference now is that these recent magazines warn women not to push for, or even expect, any commitment from men.

According to mainstream male conditioning, "getting laid" is, first, *compulsive*. The message is that a real man is always ready for sexual activity and always thinking about sex, even that men are "sex machines." In any case, it is clear that a man should act on any sexual feelings he has and that his partner too should act on his feelings. Sexual activity should come naturally and spontaneously for men. It should not require or incorporate much, or any, thought and reflection that would involve the whole male human being, including his mind.

The conditioning convinces men and women that a man's sex drive is overwhelming and possibly beyond his control. It teaches us to assume that men are somewhat irresponsible about their sexual actions. Once "it is up," he has got to do it. And the longer this conditioning has been in effect in cultures, the more it is taken to be an essential male thing, justified by questionable theories regarding testosterone and historical male aggressiveness.

Men are not only expected, but often encouraged, to be sexually active, while women are put down if they have sex outside of the narrow limits of marriage. As opinion surveys continue to show, premarital sexual activity is often considered a status symbol for males and a sign of "cheapness" for females. The most religious of people, who would counsel that sexual activity is to be saved for marriage, are quicker to forgive and down-play male sexual activity for, again, "boys will be boys." Since this is often inseparable from conditioned male aggressiveness, sexual activity is seen as just another example of male aggression, if it is not blamed on female seductive wiles. It can be controlled somewhat, but not eliminated. Women have argued with me that this is just the way men are and that's why they rape!

Recent surveys of male attitudes report that many men have performed sexually even when they were uneasy or uncertain about their partners or the surrounding circumstances. A 1999 University of Washington study reported that college men were more likely than women to report being pressured into having sex.

I have listened to numerous college age men after talks I have given on male sexual conditioning. When they spoke with me alone without their fellow males present, they often confessed about the pressure of this "compulsive" standard. They confided that they have come back to their fraternities and residence halls after a date to questions of: "Did you get some?" "Did you do it?" "Well, did you get laid?" They knew they had to portray the evening as one in which they acted on the compulsive sexuality of manhood and, as a result, they reported back to "the guys" that she "put out" for them. But in confidence they told me that not only did they not "have sex" but that they really didn't want to until they had gotten to know the woman better.

In all of this is evidence of the male fear of other men that maintains the role. The men were all clear that they certainly could not admit this to their male friends without being suspect of being less than truly male. And some even indicated that the fact that they did not want to treat a woman this way made them question their own masculinity. Of course, then, the way for a man who questions his masculinity to prove he is a "real man," is to promote compulsive sexual activity for himself and his male companions. He doesn't want their ridicule and rejection, nor to feel the internalized fear that he's less than a man.

Second, "getting laid" as defined for junior high school boys and on through the male life span is *objectifying*. It is concerned with seeing an object of sexuality in terms of bodies and body parts. No one who has listened to the conversations of boys and men around "attractive" sexual objects, can doubt that the bravado begins, and sometimes ends, with discussions of breasts and other body parts. In order to show that they are real men, they should be obvious about this interest, even in public, where real men look openly at a woman in a certain objectifying way. When Miss America walks down the runway during the swimsuit competition, she embodies best the victim of this objectification to the extent that she looks like the Barbie doll.

Third, "getting laid" is conditioned to be *impersonal*. It is best if a boy isn't otherwise acquainted with, or a friend of, the sexual object. One does not marry the girl who is the best "lay." The girl with whom one is supposed to have a permanent, committed relationship is "saving herself" for her man. "Getting laid," therefore, is not about the person. In fact, the best sex, by this criterion, may be anonymous bar sex.

I visited a university class taught by a graduate teaching assistant I was assigned to evaluate. The semester's topic was loving relationships and the discussion that day centered around the possibility of sex with a friend. The students agreed that sex ruins friendships. Of course, I had heard this before, but at that moment I was especially struck by the dichotomy between friendship and sex that the conditioning had set up in these eighty or so college students. Even adult couples who speak of their partners as their "best friends," seldom speak of their sexual attractiveness in the same breath. There seems to be something "inappropriate" about such a combination.

It is not surprising, then, that men who are having sex with their committed partner often fantasize about someone or someplace else to enhance the activity. They are actually not "there" with the person with whom they are having sex, but in some dream world where the object is not a close personal acquaintance. Many psychologists encourage such an emotional absence, and many men find it difficult to "get off" in the actual emotional presence of their long term companion.

Even more seriously, if "getting laid" is impersonal, any violence that is involved in the act can be denied. Since this act is not done with a "person" but with an object, one is not hurting a person. One is acting out a role which is masculine. And just as men create a foreign military enemy by de-humanizing the enemy with inhuman names, attributes, and stereotypes, so by thinking of the sexual object as other than a person, any consequences to the object are of less consequence. The object of the sexual act might even be referred to by a degrading name for one of their body parts.

The conditioning installs in men a fourth dimension. "Getting laid" is *manipulative and coercive*. One only has to glance at a popular TV comedy series of the 1990's, "Seinfeld," to hear about male concerns to manipulate their partners into having sex. "Did you get to first base?" "Actually, what is second base?" Men have been conditioned to believe that if they are really masculine, they can manipulate someone into having sex, "a home run!" But if they fail, something about their masculinity is on the line.

The issue is one of being a success or failure at the dominant male task. When men "force" women into having sex or claim that "she really wanted it," they are reinforcing their need to live the role, they are affirming that they are really men after all. To fail at "getting some," that is, at manipulating someone into sex, is to fail at manhood. Likewise, they should exude self-confidence regarding their ability to do this, never admitting to their fellow men that they are not very good at turning someone else on. The gender conditioning installs this need to manipulate not just as a means of proving that the male is attractive to women. There is a more crucial issue of manhood here, for the inability of that man to manipulate another into having sex means he is a failure at a dominant male task: the ability to control, coerce, and manipulate a sexual object into having sex with him.

Real women must therefore be manipulated. Actually no woman would ever submit to this role unless physically coerced or coerced by the conditioning of the system. The confusion that results in date rape and other violations of women's bodies and spirits is found here. In her conditioned role, she should never appear to want sex too early or too much. And a woman should not say "yes" too readily. She should be manipulated. By this standard, "no" is not an acceptable answer for the real man — he can and must overcome it. So, a conditioned man understands that "no" does not really mean "no." By saying "no," she is really supposed to be saying, "Manipulate me more." The conditioning teaches the man that if he is a real man she is actually encouraging him to be more manipulative and coercive. One popular woman writer has observed that the "free love" movement of the 1960's was an attempt to make women available for sex on men's terms.

If she really means "no," she will be put down for it as just "leading him on." After all, she invited him up to her room; she let him pay for the whole date; she did kiss or "make out" with him.

It is common, researchers have noted, for men to misinterpret touch. Often a casual or playful touch is taken to mean that sexual activity will follow. And that misinterpretation is in line with the layer that says real men manipulate the objects of their sexual advances into having sex. If success at "getting laid" is a goal, then a well-conditioned man finds cues to that success in any words, activities or touch.

A fifth layer of male conditioning which defines "getting a woman" is that "getting laid" is not a stage in the process of being with and getting to know someone. It is *an activity* that you *do to* the sexual object. In more "sensitive" language, it is an activity you *do with* someone. Yet, it is still an activity that begins at some point and ends at another. Conditioned men are expected to judge a date in terms of its sexual payoff. Did everything else in the evening, or did it not, result in doing "it." They will ask each other: "Did you get it." "Did you get any?" "Did you do it?"

As an activity, men are supposed to be good at "it" because the other layers of "getting laid" have told them that this is a decidedly male activity and their manhood is on the line. Men are supposed to be competent at male activities or face ridicule.

As an activity, it is one that men are taught to view as separate from all others. When it is done, it is finished. It's time to go on to other activities. Again, it is not a part of the process of life, living, and getting to know and explore intimacy with another human being. So, it does not flow in and out of a total intimacy with another. Romance leads up to *it*, but romance, touch, cuddling, are not *the* activity itself.

The sixth layer of "getting laid" follows from the fifth. As a conditioned male activity, one is not to settle for enjoyment of the process. Just as if one were producing any manufactured product, "getting laid" too must have a goal. Real men focus on results. Thus, "getting laid" is *goal-oriented*.

That goal continues on even at the beginning of the twenty-first century, and in spite of attempts by many popular sexual advisors to make women as compulsive about sex as men. It is the big "O" — his, not hers. A recent study of college students showed that most men defined sex only as intercourse. Oral-genital contact was not "sex" for the majority. It could, however, be a part of that linear movement of actions which are meant to end in the payoff: giving attention leads to kissing, which leads to petting, which leads to real "sex," that is intercourse, which leads to male orgasm which ends "sex." When the sexual object begins to move along this path, it is assumed that the end is in sight and inevitable. Even the phrase "fore-play" is a concession to this goal — all that is called "fore-play" is only the preparation for the real thing. It's what comes before *it* to get ready for *it*, but not really *it*.

The orgasm is central to conditioned manhood. One has not "gotten laid" without it. Men report that if they do not have an orgasm, their partner will conclude they are unmanly. If they should report to other men that they were sexual without having an orgasm, they will be demeaned by them. Other aspects of sexual stimulation such as massage and male nipple stimulation, researchers note, are put down as "feminine." Some men reported that if they end a date without this payoff after all the efforts and expense they put into it, they feel resentful. When popular newspaper advice columnists poll their readers for their preferences regarding orgasm and cuddling, men are generally more often than women satisfied only with "the goal."

For conditioned masculinity, a seventh layer of "getting laid" is that it is *self-centered*. This follows from general male gender role conditioning which teaches that real men are always in charge and in control of all the important spheres of life. In sex, too, men and women are to act out his agenda. If a girl doesn't submit, he will go elsewhere. How many young girls have explained to their mother, "But mom, if I don't do it, he'll find someone else."

Men have often been criticized for thinking only of themselves during sexual activity. However, selfishness is not the primary conditioned motivation for "getting laid." Outwardly, a man may appear selfish and self-centered, even arrogant. He may brag to other men about how well he lives this role. Such an outward show is how the conditioning allows him to appear to exude manhood.

So this and the other six layers deeply touch an eighth layer that pervades all of the others. "Getting laid" is believed to be *"manly."* It makes a man feel like a man and proves that he is a man.

Feelings are a key here. Male conditioning does not allow men closeness and intimacy with other human beings except in this act. All male intimacy needs are supposed to be met in "getting laid." It is okay for a man to finally feel his emotions here, and it's his sexual partner's job to make him feel like a man.

Because of this limitation, this one "activity" is supposed to be his only intimate activity. Women are allowed to experience and feel human closeness with others in numerous activities such as play, touch, caring, healing, attention, engagement, sharing goals, cuddling, dreaming dreams together, working emotionally on their relationship together, and raising children together. Since all of these expressions of closeness have been taken away from men by the male role except for this one way, and since this one way is believed to be the only way, and the way by which a man can get all other needs met, then conditioned males feel the overwhelming need for sex.

Conditioned sex, then, is not a process of expressing closeness by choice with one's whole being. It is tied to the desperate hope that it will finally make a man feel complete, and fully human. He will finally escape from the isolation of conditioned manhood which includes his homophobia. Here, in getting laid, he will finally feel like a man.

Of course, conditioned sex cannot do this, for inborn humanity and true intimacy are not so conditioned. Roles are not who we are as human beings. They are installed by fear and terror. The more "getting laid" fails to do this for him, the more he needs to "get laid" — more often, more or different partners, and more orgasms. If this partner doesn't do it, maybe another one will. And each time he seeks this in sexual activity, the man adds another bit of isolation so he is further separated from his inherent unconditioned self, and from others. The more of his hope he places in the role, the less hope he finds in himself.

He might eventually resent women for not being able to do this for him, and may come to fear women as the creatures he believes hold the power to deny him his manliness. In all this he loses hope in himself as a human being and man. He falls into a self-hate for what he does not have and cannot get. The conditioning said "getting laid" was supposed to make him feel like a man, but that is ultimately another false promise of the conditioning. He becomes more dependent than ever on the system and its coping mechanisms. Alcohol, drug use, and other mechanisms seem to help him feel better while they make money for the system.

The ninth and final dimension of "getting laid" is also crucial to manhood regardless of sexual orientation. "Getting laid" is an activity done *with a woman*, not a man. It is heterosexual. Men of all sexual orientations get this piece of the conditioning, and many gay men will attempt to live it out. Compulsory heterosexuality, as some theorists and psychologists have called it, is not a free choice. It is enforced everywhere.

If two gay men act upon their male conditioning in layers one through eight, they will be accused of doing something bad, immoral, sick, anti-God, destructive, and a threat to the family, the system and society. Society expects gay men to internalize these messages themselves and practice their sexuality as if sex is something shameful, sick, and hopelessly unfulfilling, while still acting as men are supposed to, as if it will be the answer to closeness needs. They too will rush to the goal of "orgasm" to feel the temporary thrill of conditioned closeness and to isolate for a moment from their guilt feelings. They may add chemical dependence to their sexual repertoire to "help" the feelings, hoping that sex infused with alcohol or drugs will finally give them what conditioned sex can't — an end to their isolation from themselves, their spirits, their bodies, others, and our common, complete, inborn humanity.

They will blame their sexual orientation for the fact that their experience of sex consists of the first eight layers. When two men are sexual together, they will experience double the male conditioning. They are not told that this has absolutely nothing to do with their sexual orientation. So, they will internalize the system's evaluation of them as gay men, even though the conditioning has to do with mainstream male gender role conditioning, not with homosexuality.

When the ninth layer is added to make it heterosexual sex, the conditioned male sexual role is considered good, natural, normal, pro-family, pro-society. When heterosexual men act this role out in extreme fashion at events like Mardi Gras, or in sexual violence, it is never blamed on their heterosexual orientation. This is the privileged position of the dominant sexual orientation that is used to label gay men as "dysfunctional," "perverted," or "sick" and to justify the oppression of gay men and lesbians.

The most striking example of this privileged position for heterosexuality is hardly noticed by most people. It is the fact that homosexual rape will actually be blamed on the orientation. Heterosexual rape, which is far more common, will never be blamed on the orientation. The real issue in both, however, is exactly the same: male gender role conditioning, not sexual orientation.

MORE UNEASY ALTERNATIVES

Numerous writers, particularly careful, thoughtful women observers, have pointed out something about these nine layers that ought to make all of us pause and feel this conditioning even more deeply. No matter how we might prefer denying it, we need to face the fact that the above nine layers of "getting laid" constitute a legal and moral definition of rape. To understand the issues and the depth of this conditioning, men must not shut down around this observation and go into their conditioned feeling responses. Basic mainstream male conditioning in junior high and high school is rape training. That is why psychologist John Stoltenberg, in *Refusing to be a Man*, argues that men must face this fact about male conditioning in order to heal themselves and recover their inner goodness and humanity. We all must face the reality that this is the legacy we leave our boys, and what they will have to join or fight the rest of their lives in order to cope with conditioned manhood.

What happens to the boy at thirteen or fourteen who refuses to participate in these nine layers? To his credit, he is refusing to maintain his own sense of masculinity at the expense of sexually exploiting women. Yet, he will be ridiculed, rejected, beaten and isolated. He will be asked whether he "likes girls." He will be perceived to be gay, and treated as a victim. That general putdown, "fag," which now is applied to gay men, will be the means by which he will have to reconsider his refusal to go along with "getting laid." As long as being gay is a putdown, as long as society considers it bad to be gay, the "gay slur" will be used to keep him in his place.

This is the second stage of gay oppression. It too has nothing to do with sex or homosexuality per se. It has everything to do with enforcing the male gender role, for the boy who refuses will be put down as a non-male. At this second stage of the oppression, it will be worse for him than the putdowns of a girl, for a male who does not live the idealized masculine role, is more a threat to masculinity than any girl. He embodies the contradiction. He flies in the face of the masculinity that our institutions flaunt everywhere and the system declares the highest standard of human living. He demeans the role itself by flaunting an alternative way for males to live. He is embodying the fact that there is an alternative to being "wet" and that "male" may not be best. He is a male by sex challenging everything that defines "manhood."

And "flaunting it," flaunting the alternative, is an issue for non-heterosexual people as it is for any oppressed group who steps out of mainstream conditioning. The African American who was more likely to get lynched in the post-Reconstruction south was the black man who showed an alternative to the white man. He was "uppity" and refused to live the victim role of white racism. Those who stayed in the role were a far lesser threat. Likewise, violence, threats, ridicule, and rejection will be used to try to keep a young boy in the role.

What is the least awful alternative for the boy at thirteen or fourteen? The choice he is given is to be in training to be a rapist or be a "faggot." Either he takes the oppressor role or is treated as a non-male. And this alternative is enforced through fear and terror. The victim role is denied to men but enforced onto gay men.

Women who refuse to participate are seen as lesbians. The terms "dyke" and "lesbo" are used as general putdowns for all women who do not live the conditioned female role. They eventually will be attached to women whose sexual orientation is toward other women. Some people will even minimize these women as "hating men." And the fears the system installs will be played out to further demean these women because they do not fit the ideal victim role. They receive further victimization unless they accept the victim role and respond to male sexual conditioning.

By the time we have finished high school, the conditioning we must navigate is thorough and deep. The oppression of gay men and lesbians has become the means of maintaining the gender roles. And the greatest myth today, one researcher says, is to believe that the above layers of conditioning no longer influence us. As long as it is bad to be gay in our culture, men will be afraid to move outside of, or even test the possibilities outside of, their role.

As long as it is bad to be a lesbian in our culture, women will fear stepping out of the victim role to live their lives on their own terms for themselves. When courageous women do, they may fear their success and its feelings of loneliness, or face being accused of being lesbians. Thus, some in the early women's movement worked hard to distinguish the "rights" due women from the issues of lesbians for fear of further victimization.

This look at how we raise girls and boys in our system, at the pressures and roles we install in them through fear and terror so that they stay in their "appropriate" places in the view of reality we long ago accepted, helps us understand the content and depth of that "something" that is really going on in all that we have been examining here. It gives us some insight into what needs to be changed to become human again. The task is major and multifaceted, but it is doable. The fact is that sexism, gender conditioning, and gay and lesbian oppression are all inextricably attached. No wonder it feels so hard to accept gay people.

FURTHER READING

Susan Faludi, *Backlash: The Undeclared War Against American Women.* New York: Anchor Doubleday, 1992.

Mary Pipher, *Reviving Ophelia: Saving the Selves of Adolescent Girls.* New York, Ballentine Books, 1994.

William S. Pollack, *Real Boys' Voices.* New York: Random House, 2000.

John Stoltenberg, *Refusing to be a Man: Essays on Sex and Justice.* New York: Meridian Books, 1989.

CHAPTER SIX

HOW TO BE STRAIGHT

When a gun advocacy group asked for speakers representing gay issues positively, reactions ranged from surprise to skepticism. It was highly unusual. But in fall 1998 a regional "Shooters Association" affiliated with the National Rifle Association asked the Kansas City office of the Gay and Lesbian Alliance Against Defamation to send someone to one of its monthly meetings. Its members were looking for speakers to address "Gay-bashing, its Causes and Prevention." The brutal murder of University of Wyoming college student Matthew Shepherd earlier that year had triggered their interest.

A seasoned fellow activist and friend, David Weeda, and I agreed to go. So, on a cold, dark, early November evening we set out with some uneasiness to a conservative, western Missouri suburb to address the group — after all, if we really meant what we advocated in safer contexts, we needed to speak even in what were potentially hostile ones.

As we spoke of gay bashing (David used only examples that were gun-related.), the thirty or so gun afficionados listened silently and politely. That changed during the response period when they revealed their agenda. Though they might not personally agree with "the gay lifestyle," they said, if we would support the upcoming Missouri state referendum legalizing concealed weapons, then gay people too would be equipped to fight back against their attackers.

Both of us were on the other side of that issue. So to stay with our agenda, we responded that our hope was quite different. Our goal was to change the cultural prejudices that resulted in gay-bashing and other violence in the first place.

As we said this, however, we both began to realize that, surrounded by a group of avid gun owners, the two of us actually were the most hopeful. We believed in the possibility of changing attitudes. We seemed to be the least motivated by the fear that for them made owning a gun mandatory in order to feel secure and safe.

That was quite a realization for both of us. Here was this armed group of gun advocates, all committed to living "the straight lifestyle," and dominated by a fear that needed well-armed protection. Even more, they had joined an organization to advocate for that armament as the solution to a threatening society where there seemed to be no hope for basic change. They felt the fear that underlies any of society's preferred roles, and the hopelessness about the existence of other human options that so tightens those roles around us that we believe that these roles are our only possibility. It's fear that keeps us "straight."

"Straight" is a good term for the tightrope our society wants every person to walk — rigid, up-tight, narrow, self-protectively alert, highly strung. The word is used in anti-drug support groups to describe someone not "using." It's used in anti-crime programs which hope to scare youth into a law-abiding lifestyle. It's been used as an equivalent for honesty in, "Are you being straight with me?" And it's a part of the Boy Scout's pledge to describe their standard of "morality" for real men, and now redefined to exclude gay men. It's a broad designation for everyone who fits into the conditioning at all levels. Ideally, we are to look, act, think, speak, and feel "straight."

That's what the whole system needs to keep itself going. It's the dominant role and the one we are to live. And it is a role defined by and for the system whether or not everything it includes as "straight" is actually good for human beings.

So, when we walk across the high school stage at commencement to receive our diplomas, our graduation is meant to certify more than our completion of the academic requirements of twelve years of elementary and secondary school courses. We are also certified to be well-conditioned citizens of the total cultural system of which our educational institutions are the "churches." And for those eighteen years we've been conditioned to value the "straight."

Some graduates were conditioned more thoroughly than others. Some teenagers reacted angrily or sullenly in high school to the conditioning of these teen years without knowing what it was that really bothered them.

The system worried more about those teens who resisted, who more keenly felt they were being forced to be out of touch with their in-born humanity and who were without support in those feelings. Those teens did not relish the "straight" product our system was producing in them and expressed it in anger, depression, or defiance of authority. They were considered deviants. The system responded, as we would expect, not by questioning the deep-seated conditioning but by blaming individuals, both teachers and students, and labeling them failures. For most graduates, however, the system quite successfully ingrained the rules for living inside the way of seeing reality it had defined for us.

The conditioned view of reality traced in the previous chapters and its definitions of who we are and how we are to be in the system, became so entrenched that they are assumed to be a "matter of fact." Like those wet fish, all of us swim in it and limit most of our disagreements to how best to swim, how to "make it" in this water. As a result, we seldom question these basic, culturally given definitions of who we are and what our place and purpose is in life.

The conditioning taught us to live "appropriate" roles, each role contributing to the maintenance of the total system. Even though identifying ourselves with these roles puts us further out of touch with the humanity we would freely choose and the natural needs and desires that we knew early on, the limitations the roles place on us have come to feel increasingly "natural" and "inborn." Though at times we are uneasy about this, without certainty about what is behind that uneasiness, we accept the roles and live on their terms.

The roles we are taught function as coping mechanisms in the midst of any uneasiness, pressures, and justifications. The roles are a means to cope with the "reality" that has been defined for us by the conditioning. Living them allows us to get by, to survive, and to put the best face on survival without being threatened with the violence and threats of violence, humiliation and ridicule, and isolation and rejection that will come to us if we refuse to live out and cherish the roles. "I know you are right," one male student from a large east coast city wrote me after hearing a talk. "But I just can't stand up against the roles. You don't know how much I would have to lose. I guess I'm just plain scared."

There are many roles we are supposed to live in order to fit in. They pile on top of each other until we are buried under their demands. There is a male role, a female role, a white role, a role for people of color, an upper class role, a working class role, an "adult" or "grownup" role, and on and on. There is also a heterosexual or "straight" role which is rewarded and a non-heterosexual role which is punished.

The institutions of our society profit from these coping mechanisms. We are taught that all the valued conditioned roles are attainable through our purchases, and we have come to believe this. Since we rarely are convinced that we actually measure up to the roles, but are continually told that attempting to do so is the answer to our negative feelings, our quest becomes improving upon our ability to embody these roles. Buying the next item, the next club membership, the next service, or the next status symbol, we are told, holds out the hope for further "improvement" in living the preferred role, and for the recognition and rewards society gives for doing so.

Because these roles are unfulfilling as coping mechanisms, we turn to further coping mechanisms. We can "make it" and "take" the demands of the conditioning through the use of addictive products and addictive activities which provide profits for the system. Alcohol is merely one of the most common, profit-making coping mechanisms, even for the non-alcoholic.

The system even provides us with the means to deal with what it defines as "abuse" of such coping mechanisms without challenging the conditioning itself. There are "appropriate" support groups and psychological techniques which attempt to remove individual abuse or use of addictive substances by focusing attention on the individual as the basic problem. Yet, so as not to upset the system and its view of reality, these "appropriate" techniques seldom challenge the systemic source of the underlying fears which the addiction attempts to alleviate. And these groups seem unable to say that the system itself is "crazy-making." Even less common are attempts by such support groups to challenge these unfulfillable roles. Some may even substitute more acceptable addictions. We are told that through work, diversionary activities, and the drugs approved and prescribed by the system, we can cope with the inability to "get high on life," an inability created by roles that keep us out of touch with real life.

Merely coping, through workaholism, use of mind and emotion altering substances, conditioned sex, or other means, is also ultimately unfulfilling. It doesn't get to the root of the problem.

Yet, our current system must have it this way. If any, or even all, of these coping mechanisms finally did provide the relief or connection we were seeking, we would purchase them no more. Our current economic system cannot be sustained by such contentment. It is profit-oriented and must grow at a demanding pace.

On the personal level, the more we depend upon coping mechanisms, and the more we settle for coping, the harder it is to heal the underlying issues. Coping becomes more and more familiar and comfortable. The rut we live in grows deeper and deeper until we can't see over the edges of the canyon it cuts in the earth. So as coping mechanisms, the more we live the roles, the harder it is to step out of them. We no longer see the alternatives. We believe there are none. We ridicule and dismiss those who suggest any alternatives. They are "dreamers," "out of touch," "unrealistic," "living in a fantasy world," and "just don't know how the real world works." The system fosters hopelessness and a corresponding conservative response which is self-protective and survivalist.

The more we relate to others through the roles as one role to another role, rather than as one human being to another, the more afraid we will be to reveal who we are to that other person. The other will become more comfortable with such relationships, will set up her or his relationships to us in terms of the roles, and will come to expect a role, believing also that the role is what is human. Though we might cry out for authenticity and someone who will accept us for who we really are, without masks and pretense, the entire system works to keep that from happening.

Since these roles are not human and are not freely chosen out of our complete humanity, but accepted under pressure in order to survive, they are often far from who we really are and what we would choose if we had a free, non-fear-based choice. As long as we live the roles and do not live on our own terms as who we are without the fear-based conditioning, we live as disconnected and isolated beings. The roles disconnect us from ourselves as unconditioned human beings and from others, both of our own sex and the other, as authentic human beings. In this way, these layers of disconnection constitute multiple layers of isolation as we walk through life. Our desire to deal with this disconnection and isolation, then, is an additional incentive to seek better feelings through the addictions of substance abuse or by using work and competitive play as distractions.

STRAIGHT IS NOT REALLY HETEROSEXUAL

When we look at the "straight" role the system wants all people to live, we are not looking at heterosexuality as a sexual orientation. It is important to distinguish the role from the orientation. Each is distinctly different. If a person identifies as heterosexual by orientation, that in itself does not imply a certain role. However, the system has a conditioned role that is called "straight" or "heterosexual-acting," and the system's goal is to condition every human being to live and value that role. Even people who identify as non-heterosexual by orientation, are taught to value and conform to the "straight" role.

The military for generations has recognized, for example, that gay men have served with distinction in its ranks. However, perception is important if the Marines want to be known as "a few good men." The role of straight male is to be lived out by all male Marines no matter what their orientation. "Don't ask, don't tell" is merely one of the latest versions of the straight role that the military enforces. It continues to promote an image of the military as an organization made of men who fulfill the conditioned masculine role by not exposing the real variety of ways males are.

Moreover, the increasing pressures to accept women at all levels of the military has strained the roles. Women are supposed to be victims, according to the system, not fighters. Real women do not act like men. So the role says military women should be victims of male advancements and harassment to take their appropriate place. We need to look no further than the military's own reports to hear of the existence of "lesbian bating" to keep women in their role. The female soldier who refuses the advances of male soldiers is threatened with accusations of being a lesbian and with discharge. She has stepped out of the victim role which is the woman's straight role, and the penalty for stepping out of that role is the greater violence, ridicule, and rejection of even further victimization.

If people do not live the straight role, they are placed in a victimized position. They are not only actually victimized by those who cling to the straight role, but they are expected to live a victim role themselves. Victimized people who live a victim role maintain the straight role's privileged position. They should in no way feel or express "pride" in the fact that they do not meet up to the dominant role. It is this victim role that those who do not fit the "straight" role" are supposed to live which is the subject of the next chapter.

The victimization of "gay bashing" can therefore happen to anyone not *perceived* to be straight whether they are non-heterosexual by orientation or not. According to the National Coalition of Anti-Violence Projects, a group of organizations that tracks anti-gay crimes, thirty percent of reported victims of anti-gay violence are not gay. Such "gay bashing" of people who identify as heterosexual more often goes unreported by its victims because they do not want to be suspected of being gay any more than they already have been. Witness the series of shootings in public schools around the country in 1999 and listen to how in almost every case these boys were subject to the "gay slur." These boys hoped the shootings would prove the slur wrong, demonstrating instead that they were "real men." A father of one of the young boys boasted, "At least they'll know my son isn't a fag now."

Because this role is the conditioned cultural ideal, it is not surprising that even in the gay male community, ads for "men seeking men" often say they are looking only for men who are "straight-acting" and "straight-looking." The critical point we need to understand is that it is the *role* that is valuable in a homophobic and heterosexist society regardless of one's sexual orientation.

Actually, we still know very little about sexual orientation itself. We cannot conclusively answer the question, "What is the cause of heterosexuality?" We also know very little about its actual occurrence in society. Figures are unreliable because non-heterosexuals often do not report their orientation in surveys even when they are guaranteed anonymity. Societal pressure and societally induced fear and shame have taught them that, whatever their orientation, they will not be able to hide in the dominant role and will, therefore, be treated as victims.

One current theory is that sexual orientation occurs in the same distribution as most other human characteristics. Its variations, therefore, could be plotted on a "bell curve" with people who are exclusively heterosexual a small group on one end and people who are exclusively homosexual a small group on the other end of the spectrum. If this is the case and if the straight role were removed, most people would be free to identify their orientation as somewhat ambiguous or uncertain. With the straight role in place, however, that would appear to be a frightful admission, especially with all the consequences that come crashing down on non-heterosexual, and particularly bisexual, people today.

Growing scientific evidence also indicates that sexual orientation is established early and that it is probably genetic rather than conditioned. Of course, the system that values the straight role does not want to admit such an idea. Like the systemic view of gender roles, the conditioning teaches us to see "straight" as just as natural, immutable, and inborn in human beings as conditioned manhood and womanhood. Yet sexual orientation is most likely not a choice.

Would one choose heterosexuality if it were a free choice

unconditioned by society? That question in itself is frightening to well-conditioned people, who by promoting more and harsher enforcement of the straight role on everyone can attempt to isolate from their own fear that they themselves might not have chosen heterosexuality. One anti-gay "researcher" effectively frightens his constituents by asserting that "the gay lifestyle" (defined in terms of hyper-sexual activity) must be fought because it is so appealing to human beings!

Examining the "straight" role, then, is not examining "heterosexual" as a sexual or erotic orientation. The orientation exists independent of the role, but, because of the conditioning, it is hidden under the role. Though we can identify the straight role, we know little of what it would be like to live as a free heterosexual being with the role removed. Just as the nine layers of "getting laid" installed in males during puberty are not heterosexual sex but conditioned manhood-oriented sexuality, so all that is in the straight roles of masculinity and femininity are not inherently male, female, or heterosexual but are tied, as we have seen, to the conditioned straight role. They are culturally conditioned.

What non-conditioned heterosexuality would actually look like awaits the light of day. Non-conditioned heterosexuality has not yet come out of its own closet because of the homophobia of our culture and this "heterosexism." "Heterosexism," then, is the affirmation and promotion of the straight *role* as the standard for all people, and the heterosexual *orientation* as the only valid orientation.

THE DO'S AND DON'T'S OF BEING STRAIGHT

The straight role is thereby maintained at the expense of people who identify as heterosexual as well as those who do not. As long as the role is enforced through fear and terror of appearing other than "heterosexual" as defined by the role, as long as it is considered bad not to live the role, as long as it is considered bad to be transgendered, lesbian, gay, or bisexual, human heterosexuality itself will not be livable, for we will not know what it is. People who identify as heterosexual will never be free to live their sexual orientation as long as there is fear of closeness with one's own sex and thus, as long as it is considered bad or inferior to be non-heterosexual.

Examining the straight role, then, is a probing look into what we are all supposed to look like according to the conditioning, and a look at the bondage the role places us in when compared with what we could be if our lives were based on our inherent and self-defined humanity with our actual sexual orientation, gay, straight, bisexual, or ambiguous. It is a look at the limitations enforced upon everyone by the conditioning, and how everyone is hurt by the conditioned role.

One way to examine the straight role that I use in my workshops is to ask participants to form small groups to write down every large or small act that they believe it is difficult to do in the United States because they might be treated, or thought of, the way gay, lesbian, bisexual and transgendered people are. I ask them to think about what the majority of people they know fear rather than their personal fears, because that gives the participants more freedom to explore without having to publicly identify with the fears involved.

The lists pour out. Their responses vary somewhat depending on the community and the group — a large city or a small farming community, a university town or a working class suburb, college students or professional law enforcement officers. However, they don't vary much. People know their roles even if they don't always live them because the roles have been enforced through the generations.

The actions listed, say the participants, are difficult even for those who seek to understand and support gay people. A representative list includes:

• difficulty standing in front of the "Gay and Lesbian Studies" sections at local bookstores,

- being identified with a church or other group that is known for welcoming gay people,
- visiting gay establishments or certain resort spots or neighborhoods,
- borrowing certain library books, renting certain videos, buying certain styles of music,
- going to certain movies or musical concerts,
- publicly recognizing or doing things with gay friends,
- having too many or "too close" same-sex friends,
- attending supportive events, writing supportive letters to the editor, or giving supportive sermons,
- questioning the existence of gender-defined paternal or maternal "instincts,"
- having and accepting a gay child,
- showing affection publicly (How long should a hug last?),
- moving one's body in certain ways (walking, running, dancing, standing, gesturing, laughing) or speaking in certain ways,
- looking at someone the "wrong" way or for "too long" a time,
- attending a seminar on understanding homophobia,
- raising the possibility of discussing gay issues,
- wearing certain colors or types of clothing,
- wearing certain jewelry (or too much, or too little, or in the wrong places),
- carrying or not carrying a purse or handbag,
- wearing one's hair in certain styles or lengths,
- paying too little or too much attention to fashion or one's looks,

- working out too much,
- paying too much or not enough attention to cleanliness or cooking,
- having or expressing the "wrong" feelings for one's gender,
- using the "wrong" words for things (eg., "outfit" instead of "clothes"),
- entering certain college majors or professions that are defined as gender specific (eg., engineering, women's studies, mathematics),
- having talents that are not "appropriate" for one's own gender,
- appreciating drama, dance, or ballet,
- being good or not good at sports, or paying too much or not enough attention to sports,
- driving the "wrong" car or truck,
- having certain styles of handwriting,
- having same-sex roommates after college,
- being a male who likes working with small children,
- advocating for women or other victims of society,
- being a nurturing, gentle man or a powerful, assertive woman,
- being a single parent intentionally.

Some things about the foregoing list seem immediately apparent. First, most of these questionable activities reflect the limitations of the gender roles that are part and parcel of the conditioned straight role and, thus, "real" heterosexuality. Men are not supposed to look like, act like, or be like conditioned femininity, and women are not supposed to look like or act like conditioned masculinity. At the turn of the twenty-first century, a man wearing pink is a man who is not conforming to the male gender role and a woman who is superior to men at auto mechanics is not conforming to the female gender role. The straight role is specifically defined in terms of the male and female gender roles delineated above and enforced by discrimination against those who break the rules of the role. Writer and activist Suzanne Pharr has eloquently argued that homophobia and the oppression of gay people are in reality "weapons of sexism."

THE STRICT BOUNDARIES OF BEING STRAIGHT

A second observation participants make as we view the lists taped onto the wall around us, is how limiting the straight role is. As human beings, heterosexual people as well as non-heterosexual people must give up so many possibilities in life to conform to the role so they will not be victimized by the system. Touch, creativity, vocational options, intimacies, loves, friendships, and freedom are stifled.

It seems clear, then, that the conditioned straight role prevents people from living their lives on their own terms, according to their self-chosen and unique lifestyles. It inhibits people from being in touch with an inherent and unconditioned humanity. It defines relationships with others in terms of the conditioned role, not in terms of free humanity. The symptoms are played out in issues of personal space and distance, touching, gender roles, marriage roles, lover and partner roles, the ability to heal and be healed, and the nature of participation in religion and spirituality.

The role plays out in defining even the amount of physical space that is appropriate and considered safe between human beings, in how physically close one should get to another or how close one should be when talking to another. The straight role dictates that males should be at arms length from each other. Given male conditioning to be mutual oppressors, that ensures that men are too far apart to strike each other. In its most homophobic form, it says men should greet by shaking hands. That gives a man evidence that there is no weapon in the right hand, the hand usually dominant.

The straight role for women expects them to exhibit subordinate status and vulnerability through their posture and bodily demeanor. Whereas masculine spatial use is expansive and aggressive, taking up as much space as possible for oneself, women are expected to minimize their use of space by keeping their arms closer to their bodies, their legs together, and there heads and torsos less erect, by pointing their toes inward, and using small hand gestures. Men who act similarly toward space have clearly stepped out of their straight role.

The straight male and female roles are limited further when people become partners, or husband and wife. There is growing flexibility within these roles — who does the cooking and who does the outdoor barbequing, who does the dusting and who mows the yard, or who is the main bread-winner and who should be more concerned about the problem of balancing a career and a family. Yet the culture still maintains strong dominant expectations of which we are all aware regardless of whether we heed them.

The role plays out in who becomes the authorized, authoritative healer. Men have traditionally been the doctors who can heal because the doctor is the highest position in the class system of the medical arts of which they are the appropriate members. Herbal remedies and folk medicine have historically been defined as feminine and minimized as "new age" and "unproven." Though in Europe the suppression of women midwives and folk healers, particularly older women who were not under male control, began earlier with declarations of heresy and imprisonment and the attempts to Christianize their practices, many were also killed as witches.

It also effects our own psychological and emotional healing. In addition to the hurts related to the installation of the roles that are enforced on us by the system, we are personally hurt by events of life that are beyond our control — deaths, prolonged illnesses, personal family struggles and dysfunction, natural catastrophes. With the role in place, we are kept from doing the necessary psychological and emotional exploration and healing work in personal counseling or kept from effectively participating in support groups to move us beyond the wounds and scars which these other hurts have left. The demands of the role prevent us from taking the steps we need to heal from these hurts to the extent that we are unable to get close to others, to the extent that we are in competition to be best at living the male or female roles, to the extent that we feel too vulnerable and too subject to ridicule if we speak of and feel these things, to the extent that we cannot even admit anything actually hurt us. The straight role in full force prevents progressive psychological and emotional health. It prefers that we cope even with these personal hurts by living the conditioned roles better. Exaggerated in the male, the straight role keeps males from asking for and getting help and moves them into the silence and isolation that Henry David Thoreau referred to in *Walden* when he observed that, "Most men live lives of quiet desperation."

In keeping with the straight role, religion as an organized and hierarchical institution is still predominantly a male sphere. Spirituality, the kind that includes emotions, intuitive and mystical experiences, and a sense of "relationship" with the spiritual rather than pronouncements about the Bible and the tradition, has been seen as feminine.

This is not only found in the increasingly reactionary pronouncements of the Vatican about the eternal truth of its male organizational hierarchy and its refusal to ordain women or the Southern Baptist Convention's recent affirmation of the "God-ordained" authority of the husband over the wife. One can trace the cyclical history of movements in American Christianity that, fearing the Church has become too feminine, attempt to make the church a masculine body again by restoring male leadership or "headship." Earlier in the twentieth century John R. Rice, a conservative Christian evangelist, complained that the church was being corrupted in a book entitled *Bobbed Hair, Bossy Wives, and Women Preachers*. The Promise Keepers, a late twentieth century men's movement with conservative Christian theology, represents the most recent attempt to re-masculinize Christianity by "taking back" male control of both the Church and the home.

The straight role also defines a certain, limited, pattern for sexual intimacy among people. As I have already noted when discussing "getting laid," the role dictates who should be dominant and who should be passive, who is the aggressor and manipulator of the other. In prisons, men who identify as straight heterosexuals, who outside the prison walls act exclusively as heterosexuals, are convinced that what they call "womanizing" another man, that is raping him, does not indicate they are gay. It asserts the straight male role by removing the manhood from the other man. Though the system teaches the fear that gay men are out to rape and recruit straight men, the fact is that in prison it is men who identify with the straight role who rape men who appear weaker, gay, and less able to live the masculine role. The raped men are even called "faggots" so that they are not thought of as real men.

How sexual activity should be performed, experienced, and enjoyed is limited by the role as well. The nine layers of getting laid indicate that real men should be in control and on top, the "missionary position" being the most affirming of this manhood. The role enforces the need for male orgasm by defining sex in terms of the male orgasm — all the rest is mere "foreplay" — and by the demand that men always enjoy "it."

The inability to conceive of a man being raped, of being the object of sexual advances against his will, is reassuring to the straight role. He must enjoy sex and he must always be willing to do "it." Males who have been raped suffer numerous layers of guilt and shame, for they are not taken seriously due to the terms of the straight role. After all, the role endorses rape of women. It endorses the belief that when a man does "it" "to her," he, as a real man, must be so good at sex that she really, down deep, must have enjoyed it.

People who don't fit the systemic physical, body-type, cosmetic, or beauty image of the straight role are also in danger of being victimized. A glance at American history alone shows how these images have changed, yet to live outside the current standards of male or female physical imagery is to be considered "queer." This includes "inappropriate" clothing, jewelry, physical body-types and hairstyles. As shorts on grown men became popular in the 1960's, the masculinity of men who wore them was questioned in some circles.

The increasing and renewed popularity of male earrings at the end of the twentieth century in the United States brought consternation to our culture. Living in a college town, it was clear that earrings meant little more than a thing to do, like tatoos, unorthodox hairstyles, or iridescent hair colors. But in urban, suburban, and rural areas that were more conservative, people were still asking what any male earrings meant, and especially in which ear an earring meant they were gay. They must have heard, "Left is right and right is wrong." I remember a male student who told me after going back home with earrings, that his mother's response was, "What are you doing to me?" His father was silent and distant about it.

It is seldom assumed by the straight role that the acceptable types of clothing, hairstyles, and adornment at any given time and place are simply passing and relative, like other fashions. Clothing has always been a strong indicator of social status, gender, and ethnic or religious status, keeping everyone identifiable and in her or his place. Yet at each place and time and with each different standard, clothing, hairstyles and other adornments are believed to be evidence of whether one is straight or "queer." Not surprisingly, cross-dressing has been a legally punishable offense in recent history. And some of us can remember how the hairstyles of the Beatles were taken as a sign of the end of American culture. It was a "European invasion" which to many Americans at the time meant a corruption of American values. Some even came to ask of a man who didn't fit the straight role, "Is he gay or is he European?"

THE FEAR IN BEING STRAIGHT

Another observation that stems from the lists workshop participants construct is less obvious but extremely important. Because society teaches that gay men, lesbians, and bisexual and transgendered people are scary, we might not immediately ask a key question: Who is it that we really fear when we contemplate the activities on these lists? Who are we afraid will see us standing in front of the "Gay and Lesbian Studies" section at popular, local bookstores? Who are we afraid will judge us if we publicly support equal rights for non-heterosexual peoples? Who are we afraid will ridicule men for becoming ballet dancers and hair stylists, or for merely being poor at sports? Who are we afraid will criticize and ridicule men or women who take an outward, open stand for feminist causes?

No matter how we have been taught that gay people are scary, the fact is that we are not afraid of the responses and criticisms of people who identify as homosexual or bisexual but of the responses of people who are living the straight role. In plain terms, the straight role, like the male role, is an oppressor role. Therefore, it is people who are living the straight role who enforce it on others through violence, threats of violence, ridicule, humiliation, isolation and rejection. Conditioned heterosexuals, at a fundamental level, fear each other.

This fear is thoroughly understandable, for conditioned heterosexuality, as we have seen, is a dominant program in the software installed with, and therefore characterized by, fear and terror. Remember that beginning in childhood, the role is installed through reward and punishment, violence and abandonment. It was not a free choice laid out clearly before us, but the least awful alternative available for survival in society. As an oppressor role, any personal fears that we do not live the role successfully will be acted out upon a targeted victim group — non-heterosexuals.

Since the relationships between heterosexuals are thereby conditioned to be those of oppressor to oppressor, the result is heterosexual's fear of other straight people as their potential oppressors. We are afraid to stand up against the oppression of non-heterosexual people because we fear the reactions of other straight people. What we deeply fear is that we will be treated by them in the same manner they treat non-heterosexuals. If we step out of the oppressor role ourselves to end the oppression, we might receive what we know suspected non-heterosexuals get regularly — from violence, to ridicule, to rejection. The parallels with those who stepped out of other dominant roles, such as white people and men, immediately come to mind with words like __-lover" and "hen-pecked."

People who do not act in terms of the conditioning are accused of being "faggots," "dykes," "queers." Any member of a dominant group (male, white, able-bodied, etc.) of our society may be accused of being "queer" and treated as a gay person if they stand on the side of a non-dominant group (females, people of color, differently-abled, etc). Any member of a victim group may be accused of being "queer" and "gay-bashed" for stepping out of the victim role and standing against the oppression. The terms "faggot" and "dyke" are general putdowns with clout because it is considered bad to be gay, lesbian, bisexual, or transgendered in a society enamored with the straight role.

Like all classic oppressor roles, the straight role too is self-destructive. If they live the role, it diminishes those who are heterosexual by orientation as well as those who are not. It prevents them from living their lives as they would freely. The role keeps people afraid personally to step out of the defined straight role in order to act on their own terms, from their own desires, passions and dreams, and to define their own lives, identities and activities. We are limited by it. As males, we might have otherwise been able to dance, draw, play any musical instrument, design our own living spaces, maintain close friendships, nurture the world's children, and even have been better at athletic activities because the pressure of masculinity did not destroy these interests. As women, we may have been stronger leaders, greater athletic achievers, successful scholars, and people who feel there are no limits placed on us by our sex, if we hadn't heard the messages of the role.

Again, as with all dominant roles, we are conditioned to respond to the fear behind the straight role by affirming and valuing it, and internalizing the belief that our existence is based upon maintaining the role. We lose the vision to define ourselves in any way other than the role. We feel we are the role and that taking it away will destroy us and everything we value. We act it out by enforcing it on others, or colluding with the oppression of others. One way to reconcile ourselves with a role is to justify it, to count the numbers of people who agree with it, to find ourselves in a "majority," and to convince ourselves and others that we do live it by openly enforcing it on each other. We not only collude with but join the belittling of those who question the role.

THE STRAIGHT ROLE PROMOTES OTHER OPPRESSIONS

The straight role as an oppressor role also projects the fear behind it outward by promoting or colluding with other oppressions which become attached to the role. The image of the ideal conditioned role in our culture is that of a male, white (or white-acting), able-bodied, upper class (economically successful), and adult, who is capable of "getting a woman" (heterosexual). Political scientist George Lipsitz, in *The Possessive Investment in Whiteness*, traces a strategy of combining whiteness, masculinity, heterosexuality, and patriotism together in late twentieth-century politics. The phrase "family values" invoked political and media driven images of a grouping that is white (or, sometimes, white-acting), middle class, male-dominated, and heterosexual — definitely fully "straight." Anyone who does not fit into all of these categories but appears to embody enough of the characteristics assigned to the role, threatens the masculinity of the conditioned male.

If a woman who is "his" threatens a man's masculinity by having an affair with another man, if she appears to do better what he is supposed to do well as a man, and, in particular, if she threatens his masculinity in public, the role does not allow him to say that these actions hurt or scare him and threaten his sense of masculinity. If he did so, he would surely convince other straight men that he is not a real man. Instead, the role says he should act more "like a man." He should get angry and possibly act that anger out in violence, suicide, or in a more acceptable non-violent resentment of women.

If working class men appear in some ways to be more manly, more muscled, more in touch with manly activities involving physical prowess and the earth rather than being strapped to a desk or a company in which a man feels little power, worth, or control, the "professional" male can always counter by comparing incomes. He can point to system-defined economic success to save his manhood, or he can minimize laborers as dirty. They must shower after work, while he showers before. Any oppressed group in the dynamics of an oppression has usually been stereotyped as dirtier, wilder, out of control, sexually loose, and dangerous.

The straight role promotes white racism because it is tied to whiteness in the United States. If a man of color appears to be successfully living much of the role, the minimizations take place through stereotypes ("Blacks are naturally athletic" or "Asians are naturally smart and hardworking"). These apparent ethnic compliments are actually means to explain away the individual achievements of men of color *without giving the individual any personal credit*. In a sense, their apparently superior ability to live parts of the role is due to something outside of their control while a white male's accomplishments are based on his hard work and personal talents.

In addition, the straight role's attachment to racism emasculates the males of subordinated races to minimize their threat to the dominant male model. Sometimes the ethnic group has merely been labeled feminine. "They're an effeminate race," British colonialists said of the men of India and Egypt. At other times the dignity, families, women, body parts, and role models of men of color were removed to ensure that they didn't threaten the whiteness of the dominant role.

Being too much of "a man" could cost the life of a man of color. It was the "uppity" black man, the one who was apparently making it or best living the straight male role, who would most likely be lynched in the post-Reconstruction south. And the language of white supremacist groups betrays the desire to maintain the "masculinity" of the white race. Because communities of color have also been conditioned in the straight role and want no further victimization from outsiders, it is no wonder that they may seek to distance themselves from the admission that there are gay men and lesbians within their ethnic groupings.

Since the straight role defines the ideal woman as white in appearance, traits, and style, women of color are pressured to believe what the system says of them, to adopt the look of the female straight role, and to become the best victims of males who live the straight role. The search to "get a man" for them is suppose to mean that, in spite of the strength that women of color have shown far beyond its recognition and in spite of their intuitions and real knowledge (it's women's intuition and knowledge, after all, the system says), women of color should also seek a man who is white or white-acting.

Since the system's definition of masculine success is in terms of heterosexual whiteness and since this definition is enforced economically and by every other means, women of color are supposed to burrow further into a victim role not only in terms of racism but of heterosexism and sexism. Frustrating to women of color is that men of color may try to prove to themselves how manly they are according to the systemically conditioned straight male role by "getting" the system-defined best woman, a white, or white-acting one. She is certainly not someone who stands up for the rights of women of color. In fact, only as African Americans began to accept the dominant, straight white standards for the family, manhood and womanhood, author Michele Wallace argues, did African American men and women begin to use one another as scapegoats for the effects of white racism or, in her words, they began to "resent one another."

If a gay man threatens the masculinity of the straight role, he too will suffer. The system, therefore, needs to portray gay men through the stereotype of being effeminate, that is, not meeting the male role. This image minimizes gay men and removes the threat that they may fit the straight male role better than those who identify as heterosexual males. Similar is the need to cling to the stereotype of the "butch" lesbian, to keep lesbians from appearing more feminine (better at living the victim role) than heterosexual women. The straight male role further maintains that a lesbian sexual orientation can be overcome "if they just experience a good man." The straight man's assertion of his masculinity, he feels, will make these women need him. Women who don't need him are a threat to the role.

Because the role defines the ideal male or female as adult, we are conditioned to consider children as less than fully human. We fail to listen or give credence to children and how they relate to the world. "You're acting like a child," is a put-down. "Childish," and "immature" are derogatory. "Grown-up," "mature," and "adult" are positive. Since the latter equate with embodying the roles of straight male and female, they indicate people who have settled into life in terms of the system and its conditioning. Children may be fully human, but they are not fully conditioned, and thus, by the dominant role's standards, lesser beings.

The affirmation of children's goodness, knowledge, power, and value, or even that they have rights, before they are "enculturated," "civilized," and "socialized," is a threat to the system. It is better to believe they are vacant vessels ready for adult input, uncivilized like animals, or inherently evil. And it is better to cite only anecdotes about children that support these beliefs, than to allow unsupervised and systematically unproductive play and childlike joy back into the lives of adults.

The role removes the adult's ability to play like young children in many aspects of life without competition, referees, or umpires. We are, therefore in fact, suspicious of play and pleasure. Anyone who exhibits too much joy, pleasure and unbridled fun, who does not "put it off till later," or who does not have the discipline to "control themselves" does not fit the dominant straight role with all its elements of race and sexuality, as Michael Bronski has shown in *The Pleasure Principle*. Bronski, in fact, argues that this is a fundamental attitude underlying prejudices against gay people.

Children do not naturally live the roles. Their "unruly" (outside the role) behavior touches the messages in adults that these adults received as children when they were childlike and were immediately forced to conform to adultism, modeled by the conditioned straight role.

Finally, since the role model involves physical attributes of power and control for men, and decorative beauty for women, it contributes to able-bodyism, the lessor status of people who are physically challenged. The "less than ideal" body is clearly desexualized. One need only listen carefully to complaints of thoroughly conditioned, able-bodied people when they are asked to hear and act upon the needs of the differently-abled, especially when they ask for more than a ramp.

In all of this, the role is quite fragile, for it includes within it the fear that the individual her or himself is the only one who really does not meet up to the gender role on which definitions of self, womanhood, or manhood, depend. Since no one can actually measure up to the role because it is not our inborn humanity, nor based on a human standard but on a conditioned standard, we all carry conscious and unconscious fears of failing at it. It is also not a part of the straight role to admit this failure to others. To do so will result in other people questioning and ridiculing one's abilities. It will raise to consciousness a sense of personal failure, and, without the support of others who also question the roles, it will feel isolating. Breaking the silence is not a part of the role because it would mean stepping out of the isolation and fear that keeps the role in place.

As has been noted, for conditioned men in particular, the fear that they do not meet the straight male role often results in violence against those who raise that fear in them, those who challenge one's "manhood" — women, gay men, members of other ethnic groups, foreign people, and people of other victim groups, i.e. people who represent less than the culturally defined and conditioned "manhood" ideal. A study released as late as 1999 finds that even among fifth and sixth grade boys, those who embrace the conditioned male role the most closely are most likely to describe their own behavior as aggressive.

THE STRAIGHT ROLE NEEDS HOMOPHOBIA

In addition, the conditioned straight role requires homophobia, defined as the fear of getting close to one's own sex. This fear of human closeness keeps people apart emotionally as well as physically. It prevents people from recognizing and acting upon their inherent closeness to others as human beings who, as humans, have more in common than they have differences. It prevents expressions of love and touch. The fear makes it less likely that one will discuss the variety of fears about the role themselves or other common difficulties living the roles. Homophobia is necessary to prevent the honest, open, safe discussion that would threaten the straight role's existence. It affirms that we are alone and isolated when we feel the limitations, fears, and difficulties of the gender roles.

Yet, the key to acceptance of those who deviate from the straight role is most often knowing someone as a friend or family member who is "out." For heterosexual people who attempt to leave the role, it means coming "out" to others as a heterosexual person who wants to define her or himself for themselves. Doing so will feel safe to the extent that these others are coming "out" themselves.

Likewise, people's attitudes about non-heterosexuals are most likely to change to the extent that they are close to someone who does not identify as straight. If the conditioning can portray gay people as non-human, as animals, as unappealing beings far removed from "respectable" humanity, this will prevent people from attempting to get close to gay people. Picturing gay, lesbian, bisexual, and transgendered people as inhuman and unappealing goes beyond maintaining discrimination against them. Such portrayals have as their larger goal the maintenance of the security of the straight role.

THE STRAIGHT ROLE RUINS SEX

At the same time as it denies what is a natural human closeness, the straight role defines closeness and intimacy almost exclusively in terms of patterned, genital, heterosexual sexual activity. This is the only activity in which men are supposed to get or feel intimate. Women are supposed to respond to genital sexual activity as if this too is their means of getting close to that exclusive male being who is their man.

The idea that genital activity takes place in same-sex relationships, threatens the role, for the homophobia of the role says true intimacy can only exist and be expressed between a man and a woman. If it is otherwise, the role is threatened. And the way to deal with this threat is to claim that there cannot be true closeness between people of the same sex, and to portray their genital sexual activities as something wholly other than loving, tender, caring, intimate, or even human. It must merely be deviant "sex," more like that of animals or other "subhuman" creatures. Attacking gay people around their sexual activity is directly a function of the straight role and the demands of the nine layers of stress involved in "getting laid" as defined by the role.

The pressure the straight role places on sexual feelings is overwhelming. Like other emotions, sexual feelings are neither good nor bad but feelings to be felt. It is a human choice whether to act on one's feelings. Acting on a feeling, however, is often a way not to feel the emotion any longer. Making any decision over any complicated issue, for example, often feels better than feeling confused. The action distances one from the emotion by substituting acting for feeling.

In such a way, the straight role says we should act upon sexual feelings in order to feel human closeness. Since such feelings are at best fleeting, and cannot provide closeness, one response is to act on them more. The result may be sexual compulsions and addiction. In fact, Anne Wilson Schaef argues that three of the most common addictions in U.S. society, sex, romance, and relationship addictions, are not only the results of a child's personal experiences in their homes but also due to this larger societal conditioning. Society promotes and thrives on these "process" addictions. Yet she identifies them as ways for both men and women actually to "escape from intimacy."

Since it is attached to straight, gender role conditioning, conditioned heterosexuality in men couples violence and sex. Though writers on male sexuality often focus on this violence in terms of the "rape training" that is mainstream, male, gender role conditioning, there is another element of male sexuality that propels both the confusion and the violence.

The conditioned view says that men are supposed to be naturally good at sex. They are are also supposed to be able to get all the sex they want as well as be the ones who are in control of any sexual situation. If these are not apparent, men will fear that it is also apparent that they have failed manhood. Issues like "erectile dysfunction" are more to conditioned men than a medical concern and Viagara is more than just a physical medicine.

Though men are not supposed to talk about this, the aroused male organ is extremely vulnerable. It is vulnerable to physical assault, to criticism, and to rejection. It can be considered "too small" or its obvious condition, desires, and message can be rejected. The conditioned role makes men understand any of these as a criticism of their virility where large sexual organs, the ability to manipulate others into sex, being in control, and goal orientations reign.

The conditioned male feels this threat and needs to assert manhood in some action which stops these feelings of fear. "The best defense is a good offense." Hurt and fear are unacceptable to the conditioned male role, but anger is "masculine." Conditioned manhood can be desperately recovered through rape, sexual abuse, molestation, violent forms of pornography, or violent, impersonal sexual aggression even with a willing partner. In the process, a conditioned man can again feel close and "manly." Rape is an inexcusable act of violence, but it is an act of desperate conditioned, straight masculinity which affirms the conditioned straight role.

If closeness is defined in genital sexual terms, then any closeness with a member of the same sex raises fear. As long as it is bad not to live the straight role, that is, as long as it is considered bad to be transgendered, bisexual, lesbian, or gay and as long as the content of that fear is that same-sex closeness might be or might become sexual, then closeness will be impossible. It will be accompanied by the fear that if one should enjoy closeness one might either be homosexual or be perceived as homosexual. As long as it is believed to be wrong, sick, abnormal or perverted to be homosexual, as the straight role teaches, this fear will keep one from same-sex closeness.

In specific terms, *any* fear one has about getting close to one's own sex will become the content of one's homophobia. This will include fears regarding the early stereotypes of gay men and lesbians that the system taught us. It will include what we saw would happen to someone who was perceived to be too close and was assumed to be gay or lesbian. It will include our own experiences when we felt we crossed some line of "appropriate" closeness and the emotions associated with it, or we remembered having feelings, sexual or not, of connection and closeness for someone of the same sex that the conditioning told us we shouldn't feel. Like that little preschool girl mentioned above, we may have been taught to fear hand holding. We may wonder how long a hug should last with a member of the same or other sex. As we hug, we may hear messages like: Am I enjoying this too much? If so, what does that mean about me? Will he or she think I'm gay or coming on to him or her? What will other people think if they see this?

It will include the fear (especially for men) that a gay person will "come on to me." "Straight" people will be unable to react to such an advance proportionately and in a relaxed manner, with a "Thank you, I'm not interested," and with appreciation for the fact that another human being found them attractive. Instead, the fears will rise about being perceived to be gay and the possibility of being similarly victimized. What did I do that made them think I was gay, lesbian, or bisexual? Oh no, am I giving off gay vibes? Do other people think this? Since we are conditioned to believe it is bad to be gay and we know what happens to gay people, I better do something right away to prove to myself and to show other people that I am not. Gay bashing, and gay jokes, or other gay putdowns come in handy. They help me personally and publicly do something so I do not feel the fear and terror of questioning who I am or of being on the receiving end of the prejudices and oppression gay people receive.

A small, but interesting, study published in 1996 by researchers at the University of Georgia provides the first scientific evidence that the fear, anxiety, discomfort, and hatred that males living the straight role have toward gay people may actually be a result of repressed homosexual urges which the person needs to deny, or unconsciously fears. In a controlled study of university students, those who were most anti-gay showed significant arousal when viewing a video of male homosexual sex.

In addition, this homophobia attached to the straight role is another element that supports the manner in which we advertise products and create needs for them. It enables the economic system to further exploit the feelings of isolation and separation by selling products to people to make them "feel" close to others in terms of conditioned definitions of closeness. Every product not only helps one appear to embody the straight role of male or female, but promises that feelings of closeness to other human beings will result from its purchase and use. Another false promise.

THE STRAIGHT ROLE EXPLOITS WOMEN

The straight role functions in one more way. Conditioned heterosexuality promotes sexism and the exploitation, objectification, scape-goating, and blaming of women by both sexes. It keeps people from standing up for equality for women. Should anyone stand up against the victim role for women, they will be accused of being gay or lesbian. This makes it difficult for men to champion women's causes because doing so is not only stepping out of the male role, but it is devaluing the straight role and suggesting alternatives. So men who stand up against the oppression of women are accused of being gay. Likewise women who refuse to accept the victim role in sexism are accused of being lesbians. The role itself keeps one in the role and keeps one supporting it.

Living as a straight human being according to the societally approved and conditioned role is on the one hand easy. It allows us to cope with the conditioning rather than challenge it and to make it through life without facing our fears.

Examining the straight role is complicated because "straight" is dominant, mainstream, accepted as just the way things are meant to be, enforced through fear, and puts us out of touch with our inborn humanity and the freedom to be who we might otherwise be. It keeps us all apart and portrays itself as enforcing its fears and distress on people who by sexual orientation are not heterosexual. It is taught to us regardless of sexual orientation and maintains a hold on us which at the end of the twentieth-century has made U.S. society the most uptight, homophobic society in history.

But it is conditioning, not destiny. It can be un-learned by very courageous people who want something better for all of us, themselves included. Living the role is far from brave. It's rewarded.

Frustration with such a straight life is more common than we hear, but seldom understood for what it is. Most often we blame the discontentment on ourselves personally because we have not lived up to the roles that society says will give us the contentment and connection we seek. The good news is that this can change and there are people who are attempting to do that.

There are others though who because their sexual orientation is not heterosexual, are supposed to live as victims of the conditioning. To understand these roles more fully, our next task is to look at that victim role that people who identify as gay, lesbian, bisexual, and transgendered are conditioned to live so that the system will grind on without them threatening it. Then we will look at dismantling both roles. No one will be free until everyone is free: heterosexual, homosexual, bisexual, transgendered or uncertain.

FURTHER READING

Keith Boykin, *One More River to Cross: Black and Gay in America.* New York: Anchor Books, 1996.

Michael Bronski, *The Pleasure Principle: Sex, Backlash, and the Struggle for Gay Freedom.* New York: St. Martin's Press, 1999.

George Lipsitz, *The Possessive Investment in Whiteness:*

How White People Profit from Identity Politics. Philadelphia: Temple University Press, 1998.

Suzanne Pharr, *Homophobia: A Weapon of Sexism.* 2nd ed. Berkeley: Chardon Press, 1997.

Anne Wilson Schaef, *Escape from Intimacy: Untangling the "Love" Addictions: Sex, Romance, Relationships.* New York: Harper San Francisco, 1989.

Michele Wallace, *Black Macho and the Myth of the Superwoman*, London: John Calder, 1979.

Chapter Seven

How to Be Gay

What about people who are not heterosexual by orientation? They know they are not "straight" in that crucial sense required by the "straight role," and they're reminded of that fact daily. They fall in love with, are passionately attracted to, and want to express themselves sexually with the same sex. So they are not "straight" by definition.

Yet to keep the straight role dominant, gay people are conditioned to accept another role that maintains "straight' dominance. They are supposed to be victims of the straight role not merely as acted out on them by straight people and society's institutions, but as victimizers of themselves. They should put themselves down, and value the straight role at their own expense.

When personal ads placed by men or women seeking a same-sex relationship specify that they prefer someone "straight-acting" or "straight-looking," the ads are evidence that gay men, lesbians, and bisexual or transgendered people are acting out of the societally conditioned "victim role" that corresponds to the "straight" role. They are valuing each other as if the "straight" role is best.

When gay men complain that the only thing gay men are interested in is sex, they are living out of the same victim role. They are defining the group to which they themselves belong in terms of the dysfunctions found in the "straight" role. They are buying into the shaming of sexuality in general and their sexuality in particular, and are hoping to hide it altogether.

When lesbians list everything they hate about lesbians, they are speaking out of the victim role. They are assuming the straight role's teaching that their problems somehow have to do with their sexual orientation rather than systemic gender conditioning for women.

When gay people work to play down the fact that a significant part of being homosexual is sexuality, just as it is in heterosexuality, they are living out of that victim role. They are trying to appear as "straight" people, to appear as if they don't have same-sex genital activity, and are seeking their worth in sexual values defined by the "straight role."

When they say, I wouldn't choose to be gay if I had a choice, they are expressing the self-hate of the victim role. They are accepting the dominant "straight" cultural myth that "straight" would be the better choice for them if they had a free choice in the matter.

When they argue that the reason they deserve to have the rights straight people have is because they don't have a choice and were "born this way," they are arguing from the conditioned victim role. They are saying that they "couldn't help" their inferior sexual orientation and that is why "straight" people should accept their condition.

Identifying a Victim Role

The role that the dominant teaching of our society wants non-heterosexual people to live is a classic victim role. In the theoretical terms of the dynamics of any oppression, people who are conditioned into any victim role are conditioned by the fearful means discussed in chapter two to believe at a deep, emotional level:

1 that the dominant role is the ideal that is preferred, natural, human, moral, healthy, pro-society, pro-human, pro-God;

2 that people who live this dominant role are the ones who correctly define, and are most qualified to define: a) the oppressor and victim roles, b) what oppression and prejudice really are regarding the roles, and c) what values go with the roles;

3 that those who are not a part of the dominant group should live to emulate that dominant role as closely as possible, no matter how difficult doing so might be for these outsiders;

4 that there is something inferior about members of the non-dominant group that will make it impossible for them to actually succeed at the dominant role;

5 that this inferiority consists of everything that makes members of the non-dominant group "inherently" different from members of the dominant group who can easily act out their "inherent," better characteristics;

6 that anything in the non-dominant group that does not match the dominant role should be hidden or "corrected" if possible because it is inferior, shameful, unnatural, immoral, inhuman, dirty, unhealthy, uncivilized, destructive of society, and anti-God;

7 that the successful embracing of this victim role means that members of the non-dominant group should enforce the victim role on each other.

The system's conditioning about gender superiority teaches that boys are best, that conditioned boys living the straight role are even better, and that girls should recognize, identify with, and live in terms of their inferior status. In the same way it teaches everyone that heterosexual is best and that heterosexual people living the straight role are even better. At a foundational level it also conditions gay men, lesbians, and bisexual and transgendered people to believe straight is best and that they will be better to the extent that they live the "straight" role. If they can't, it only proves that there is something wrong with them.

In one sense, the victim role that corresponds to the idealization of "straight" (what some have called heterosexism) is unlike the conditioned roles of racism, and sexism. The straight role is a place where people of homosexual or bisexual orientation can more easily hide than people in other oppressions. A person of color has a difficult time hiding their obvious skin color for, no matter how our culture claims to be "color blind," it is not. "Color blind" in this sense, is impossible unless we are completely blind. A woman may have a difficult time hiding her sex if it is obvious that she has physical features associated with female biology or exhibits characteristics of the conditioned definition of femininity. But a gay person can hide, can deny that she or he has the systematically defined inferior sexual orientation, by denying it to themselves personally, denying it to others through living a clandestine life, or both.

In this cover-up, the gay person is actually closer to the heterosexual person who can decide when to live a straight role or when not to do so. Not surprisingly, many "liberal" heterosexual people find greater freedom to be themselves in the presence of gay people because they are not afraid to step out of the straight role in the presence of gay people. The harder task for heterosexual people is doing so among people who are committed to living the straight role. It's hard because they fear that the oppressor element of the straight role discussed in the previous chapter will come down on them if they challenge the straight role with "straight" friends, acquaintances, or family.

It is true that a person of color learns quickly how to "act white" in order to move up the corporate or social ladder. They learn what they must give up or hide to do so, what must be said to or hidden from white people, and how they must separate from many other people of color. Yet the "victim role" of heterosexism differs from that of other prejudices and oppressions. There is a greater element of choice as to how and when one will live as a person of the non-dominant sexual orientation. That choice can differ moment by moment depending upon the immediate environment in which one finds oneself. One can be "out" in personal social settings with some friends and not others, and still be in the proverbial closet at work or with one's family.

So, the task of identifying how gay people are supposed to live the victim role, given the systematic conditioning of the institutions of our culture, is more complicated because it is easier to hide the fact that one's sexual orientation differs from the dominant one. And hiding one's sexual orientation is one way to live the victim role. One hides because one feels like a victim of straight people, and by hiding one affirms and endorses the straight role to the larger society.

As we examine one example of societally conditioned "victim roles," the "gay" role, it is important to emphasize that the role is separate from two other factors in the lives of homosexual and bisexual people. First, just as the "straight" role is completely separate from a heterosexual orientation, the "gay" role, as any conditioned victim role, is separate from homosexual or bisexual sexual orientations. The role has nothing inherently to do with sexual orientation. No one is naturally a victim. Human beings must be conditioned into this role too.

A second distinction which must be clear is that the victim role non-heterosexual people are expected and conditioned to live is different from the well-documented fact that gay, lesbian, bisexual and transgendered people have been, and are still, victimized by our culture. Many in our society are in as much denial about this as they are about the on-going realities of racism and sexism. It takes brutal murders and destruction of gay people and their property to get media attention. Yet this actual victimization is what clearly installs and enforces the victim role in members of victimized groups.

The distinction being made here is that one can be victimized without living the victim role or one can live the victim role when one is not being victimized. Whereas people in the dominant groups must also be conditioned through fear and terror, the result is that they are conditioned to live an oppressor role with all its privileges and dominance. Victimization is real, and that makes the victim role a fearful role to leave. But being a victim of oppression is not the same as accepting the psychological, emotional, mental *role* of the victim which adds the element of self-victimization to it.

The Victim Role Feels Safer

People conditioned into a victim role have learned that, though they will be victimized even if they live the victim role, the level of victimization will be less than the violence, ridicule and rejection they might experience if they step out of the victim role to live their lives on their own terms. If they reject the role, they learn, they will be threatened with further victimization. People of color are supposed to "stay in their place" and not "flaunt" their ethnicity in the midst of a culture that flaunts whiteness and its privileges. Women are supposed to live the straight role of femininity by not standing up for their inherent intelligence, equality, and self-definitions of who they are and what makes them worthwhile. They are to defer to the male standards of our culture.

In the same way, non-heterosexual people are supposed to stay in their place and not "flaunt their sexuality." They are to stay in a closet while the straight role and its conditioned sexual patterns are "flaunted" at every turn in movies, romantic songs, on television, in most magazines, and in other elements of popular culture. A victim role, then, is imposed through fear of further victimization for anyone who steps out of the role and who, by doing so, gives evidence of their health and power and rejects the definitions and limits of the system. Fear of further victimization keeps non-dominant groups in the role. Since the victimization is real, that fear is a real one.

In addition, the victim role is a refuge because it is familiar. The ease of acceptance of any victim role by an adult is due to the fact that it is so deeply recognizable, even to the point of feeling comfortable. It is one of the early roles human beings learned to accept while children.

Accepting the victim role for the child was the least awful alternative available in a culture based upon the beliefs that children are property, not fully human, born evil, "uncivilized," meant to fulfill adults' needs, or at best empty vessels into which adults must pour humanity. Children who did not accept their inferior status had everything to lose from the adults around them. This is, to be frank, the oppression of children, courageously identified by child psychologists such as Alice Miller. When this is combined with the culture's lack of support for parents through misinforming them about children and their needs, through the mystification and justification of the conditioning the parents themselves received as children, through lack of support for parenthood outside the system's limits, through idealization of the unhealthy and restrictive nuclear family, and through the promotion of a lifestyle that requires that attention be taken away from people (especially children) and placed onto what benefits the economy, it ensures that familiarity with the victim role is installed early.

Systemically, the victim role functions to keep people and institutions in place. It does so by conditioning those who are victimized into living so as not to threaten the dominant structure and its hierarchy of oppressors and victims. Victimized people are conditioned to live, and expected to live, the victim role in order not to "disturb the peace."

Liberation movements disturb the system. So they are accused of "stirring up things" and "creating trouble." It is a popular response to the empowerment of any victim group to blame them for causing the problem. A common reaction to the women's suffrage, civil rights, migrant workers' rights, women's equality, and gay liberation movements was to blame "those people" for bringing up the issue and "causing trouble and division." One function of "blaming the victim" is to keep people in their victim role.

SEEING LIFE THROUGH THE LENSES OF THE VICTIM ROLE

The first element of the victim role that those who are victimized are conditioned to internalize is the approach to life which interprets all events though the confident, ever-present expectation that they are about to be victimized. Should they ever begin to feel that there is a chance that their lives would be better either immediately or "in the long run" if they were to step out of the role, stand up together against the real victimization, and contend for their rights, they might actually begin to step out of the role. That would upset the balance of society. It would require those in the dominant group to have to question and reexamine their positions and adjust to changes in the structures.

Rightly so, gay people have had to look over their shoulder to be aware of what will come at them. They are not to be blamed for doing so. But there is a difference between being alert and aware and always expecting hurt.

It is important to hear what the great leaders of liberation movements such as Mahatma Gandhi and Martin Luther King, Jr. have had to preach again and again: the *fear* of oppression can be more powerful than the oppression itself. It can disable people so that they don't think clearly about how to handle, defuse, or confront the actual oppression that takes place when it begins.

Expecting to be hurt, and feeling that there is danger all about, is understandable. There are enough examples of death, pain, and rejection to make it feel as if all human contact will be that way. There are enough examples of lack of support from organizations and from authorities that support people who live the straight role, such as the church and the police, to make people believe that it seems safest just to act as if one will be victimized. Religious organizations have turned gay people away or forced them to deny their loves. Police and courts have taken gay people's issues less seriously, completely dismissed them, or held gay victims of abuse and violence responsible for it.

No wonder gay people feel safer seeing victimization when what people may actually be doing is struggling to understand and overcome their own upbringing. There are enough examples of rejection, competition, ridicule, and fighting for turf within gay communities to convince one that rejection and ridicule is par for that course too. Expecting to be mistreated and acting as if one will be, then, are protective measures to prevent any future hurts. They are understandable and also dis-empowering.

This expectation of victimization blocks a human being's analytical, creative, and intelligent abilities. These abilities are what enable one to respond effectively and to challenge the actual nature and amount of discrimination taking place at any present moment. Beginning with the expectation of victimization is like seeing through a fog at best or coming up against a wall that keeps one from seeing beyond it. It is reacting out of fear, a fear that is triggered by actions, words, sensory stimuli, and thoughts that resemble those in the past that actually did hurt. The fear surrounding those past memories prevents one from seeing what is actually happening in front of a person now, at this moment. In so doing, it prevents one from preparing adequately for the range of possibilities in an event and from reacting proportionately, effectively, rationally, creatively, and safely to what is happening now.

For those who are conditioned to live the victim role, this disabling fear rises because it is based in the victim role and installed through early past hurts. It is not merely a reaction to the facts of the present experience. The system needs this reaction so that gay people do not act effectively to end the systemic nature of the oppression itself. They are supposed to act ineffectively, not out of the realization of their power and intelligence. The victim role tells them to wait till straight people "get it" and then change, as if those who live the straight role will sort of come to it on their own without seeing alternatives to the straight role. The system also needs this gay victim role to maintain homophobia, for the role expects rejection and ridicule, and thereby, like a self-fulfilling prophecy, acts in a way that promotes and enforces homophobia and the separation that homophobia reinforces.

I was standing outside a campus building which housed my office. A few students were talking with me about the class in Eastern religions we had just finished. Two male students walked by holding hands and one of my students asked, "What do you think about that, Professor?"

Now there are many answers I could give to that question, depending upon how I interpreted its intentions and if I expected victimization. I could have responded out of a victim role with preaching, scolding, shaming, or silence. I could have assumed certain intentions, such as that the student is seeking to victimize gay people. But, the fact is, I did not know what the student's intentions were. We seldom really know, though our past fears may make us take the guesses of a victim.

I responded, "I think everybody should hold hands. If everybody held hands, we couldn't hit each other, or shoot each other. We could help each other cross the street just like when we were all supposed to hold hands in kindergarten."

Such a response, I believe, touched the real issue of homophobia in a relaxed and creative way. It assumed that the words that were spoken by the student in his question said exactly what the student meant. And the somewhat playful answer harkened back to childhood before we were conditioned to ask whether holding hands with our friends meant we would be put down as "lesbos" or "fags."

At the beginning of an "Understanding Homophobia in Faith Communities" workshop, two men identified themselves as members of the modern, Evangelical Christian men's movement called the Promise Keepers. It was immediately obvious that most people in the room froze when the men revealed this. I would guess that many of the attendees were expecting something negative because of what they had heard or experienced about a movement whose leaders' teachings fit the straight role well and are homophobic.

The challenge was not to respond out of the victim role (even though there are many reasons to expect to hear victimization). One can choose at such a point in time whether to treat these men as human beings or only as members of a movement. One can choose to be relaxed and observe what is actually going on in the room about one or expect something bad as inevitable. In fact, the men listened and willingly participated in the processing of the workshop which turned out to be an eye-opener for them. They went away with a new understanding of the issues. There was no confrontation. There could have been, but I, thankfully, did not assume its inevitability and remained free for a proportional reaction to whatever would happen.

COMING OUT

For gay people, no issue illustrates these victim expectations more than the expectations they often have when they "come out" by revealing their sexual orientation to friends, family, co-workers, and anyone with whom they must do their everyday activities. It is common to assume reactions of rejection, ridicule, and hurt.

That can and does clearly happen, as far too many personal experiences attest. Parents do turn their backs on their children. Some friends do pull away. And some job situations are compromised or lost due to the reactions of supervisors and co-workers. That's why no one has the right to tell others how or when to come out. The time, place and manner of doing so is a personal decision. Rob Eichberg's book, *Coming Out: An Act of Love*, is therefore an insightful guide for coming out without assuming a victim role.

Certainly, the first step out of the victim role is to begin the process of coming out. But one can come out with the expectations of the victim role or as a part of one's own growth and through one's own strength and integrity. A person can come out knowing that people will react out of their own conditioning but not assuming she or he will be rejected. If gay people come out on their own terms they will give those to whom they come out the chance to process the revelation. They will realize that some people may need their whole lifetime, and they will have to be given all the time they need without having them in one's life. Some people may just need time. Other people may need reassurance that this revelation does not change anything on the part of the gay person toward them. Whatever the person coming out decides, they get to choose how to observe and relate to the people who react.

They also get to reject "victim role" teachings that the reactions of other people to the "coming out" are the fault of the gay person, that she or he did it "wrong" or ineloquently, that it is their orientation that is the problem, or that if the person coming out were different that would make it all better. To step out of the victim role is to realize that not coming out was saving those others from their own homophobia and their own need to confront the straight role in their lives. It is to accept the fact that, no matter how they react, it is time they faced their own conditioning whether they choose to do so or not. If gay adults need the approval of others, particularly heterosexual people and parents, to live their lives, then they are living as a victim of those others' assessments of them and not in terms of their own definitions of who they should be. They are living other people's lives, not their own.

Because of the depth of the conditioning and its hurts, it usually takes some personal work in counseling and support groups to begin to distinguish the real victimization from the victim role. And in the process, victimized people do not need a further sense of guilt for living the role. They did not ask for it, don't deserve it, and were not born with the victim role somehow inherent. It is all cultural conditioning. Yet, those who have been victimized in the past have not lost the ability and power to decide never to live the role of the victim again.

Without the automatic expectation of victimization that is part of the conditioning of the victim role, one can observe what is actually going on and determine whether one is in fact in a real and present, personal danger. One can then take complete charge in the present of one's own space, protection, and safety. One can make decisions as to when to risk and to take a chance. There is a time to stand up and say "Hell no, we won't go!" There is a time to wait, to listen carefully, and to decide that the real danger in the present is not worth the risk. Making such decisions consciously is rejecting the victim role. Making decisions takes back control of one's life.

A life lived in expectation of victimization does not expect people to be human beings who may be misinformed and moved by their own fears when that really is the case. It does not see when others are caught in *their* misinformation, *their* conditioning, and *their* fears, and it ultimately blames oneself for the issues of others. Because it does not begin with the present events in the actual situation being faced, the victim role response does not note what is really going on when people deviate from their humanity into the conditioned roles that are the real threat. The victim role is not pro-active but re-active, even over-active, protecting itself from the expected victimization.

Few current leaders are doing more to lead gay people out of the victim role in the struggle for equal treatment than Reverend Mel White, author of *Stranger at the Gate*. White attempts to apply the non-violent "soul-force" principles of Jesus of Nazareth, Mahatma Gandhi, and Martin Luther King, Jr. to the struggle for ending the oppression of all people. In doing so, he continues their attempts to press victimized people to focus on what is actually going on in the minds of the oppressors. The oppressors are "victims," he says, of misinformation and fear.

"Soul-force," as an approach to life, is itself a rejection of conditioned responses to life's events. Its methods contradict standard conditioning, both the angry, macho, violent, competitive posturing, and self-defensive stance of conditioned masculinity as well as the victim role of any victimized group. It speaks in terms of healing, self-empowerment, recognizing the level of hurt in humanity (whether friend or enemy). It responds not out of past hurts and their expectations, but in a manner that contradicts, even offends, conditioned manhood.

Yet to those who are unable to step out of the victim role, those for whom activism is belligerent, angry, embittered, and possibly functioning as an addiction, White appears to be capitulating, playing up to the enemy, and failing to fully demonize them. The angry reactions of gay protesters who stood with rabid, anti-gay protesters against White's attempts to non-violently coerce fundamentalist Christian minister Jerry Falwell into toning down his rhetoric about non-heterosexuals in Lynchburg, Virginia in 2000, expressed the anger and hurt of victimized people who preferred angry, even abusive, actions in return.

Angry reactions are understandable, given the long history of religious abuse perpetuated by Christian and other religious leaders. Why one would expect better, is certainly a good question. Whereas White is affirming that society has to create a bigot through fearful, hurtful conditioning, others, responding out of the fact that these people continue to hurt gay people, assume that these people are irreformable and will only further victimize gay people if given the chance. To them, White's call seems to illicit further abuse. For White this "soul-force" approach is actually an empowering reevaluation of everything that is happening. It turns the attention to a real problem — the issues of the abusers themselves, what the system did to them, and their need for healing. It is self-empowered and outside the victim role which gay people are supposed to live.

I repeat, no one who has been victimized can be blamed for expecting further victimization. Victimization has often been the pattern in the past and it has hurt. But living with the constant expectation of more victimization limits the life of gay people, keeping them from experimenting with the possibilities that are available.

People who step out of the expectation into the present "share and check" the responses of others, take a step and note the reactions. They are free to observe the actual reactions of others, and mentally present enough to judge the real effects of the reactions on them. In addition, they don't have to share everything out of some guilt, desire for acceptance, or desperate need to do so either. They can make rational choices about sharing. The person living outside the victim role never shares what she or he perceives will bring actual victimization unless it is also empowering.

Those of us who are conditioned into the oppressor role love to speak of "the victim mentality" of victimized people as if those people have not actually been, and are not actually being, victimized. In this way, people who are committed to the straight role can deny any of their own patterns of victimizing others, their own fears about how they themselves might deviate from the straight role, and their own feelings about how they were treated as they grew up in the culture. It is easier to act out one's hurts through the mistreatment, blaming, and scapegoating of others than to face and feel the hurts of the past which turned human beings into people who live oppressor roles. Blaming others is a way to cope with the hurts from their pasts, but it prevents the healing of the effects of those hurts in the present.

A call for the victimized to step out of the victim role is not a call for them to deny that they have been victimized. It is an opportunity to examine what's really going on, the actual dynamics of the systemic conditioning and its oppressions. It is an opening for creating strategies to change society so as to refuse to be victimized again.

Outside the victim role one recognizes that there are no human enemies. The enemy is the system humans have created and maintained. Yet many gay people still prefer to embrace the system by valuing the straight role and not creating their own place in life, a place which also expects "straight" people to act like unconditioned human beings. They want to conform to "straight" as much as possible, not realizing the damage this is doing to everyone and what they must give up of their humanity to conform.

THE SELF-HATE OF THE ROLE

Internally, the victim role includes deep self-hate. This self-hate is actually an internalization of the system's misinformation about the victimized group. The victim role accepts the valuation that the dominant group has placed upon the victimized group, for this dominant message comes from everywhere and soaks in.

It may take the form of media portrayals as documented in the history of cinema in the film *The Celluloid Closet*. The documentary traces the history of negative portrayals of gay men and lesbians in the movie industry, images that pictured for many who they were. It may take the form of comedy which plays on the stereotypes of gay men and lesbians. It may be the internalization of the messages of religions which condemn non-heterosexual people or say they "hate the sin but love the sinner" while defining the "sinner" almost exclusively in terms of "the sin." It may be an internalization of any stereotypes so that one's "gaydar" goes off when someone who fits the stereotype arrives. It may pressure non-heterosexuals to change their "lifestyles" when they come out in order to fit in. Then as they act out the stereotypes they will set off that "gaydar" in those who rely on the stereotypes.

The content of this self-hate is anything that keeps gay people from living in the settled, relaxed belief (with no need to defend it in anger or arrogance to others) that they are good, whole, and complete. Few counselors and workshop leaders who have worked with gay people would deny that transgendered and bisexual people, lesbians and gay men carry around a deep sense of being flawed, incomplete, and dirty. This self-hate creates the belief that in fact "I am what the system has defined me to be: not a real man, not a real woman, not even a full human being, not normal, not worthy, not capable, etc." It is this self-hate that leaves one with the sense that somehow, at some hidden level one really is "bad," "broken," "incomplete," "damaged," "sick," in search of a lost father or mother, "lazy," "ugly," "incapable," "unintelligent," "immature," "less than human," and on and on.

Part of the conditioning is to blame any psychological dysfunction in the life of gay people on their sexual orientation. Whereas conditioned gay male sexual activity is the result of the standard male conditioning which all males receive and which is doubled because it involves two males, society blames it on gay male sexual orientation. And many gay males believe that it is their orientation that is flawed in this way, not the systemic male conditioning. If they were to fully realize that the problems they encounter in their personal life and relationships which often get attached to their sexuality really were due to systemic male gender conditioning, they would change the system with its gender conditioning and demeaning of all that is "non-male." They would certainly not try to blend into it. To believe the problem is you and your orientation is accepting the victim role.

Lesbians, like most women, have been conditioned to relate in relationships as mutual and competing victims who place less value on women's valuations of one another. Not present in their relationship is the male approval they have been conditioned to feel they need, and women's approval is of less value in our culture. As one lesbian friend said to me, "That's why we can't feel good about ourselves. We're always looking for approval and validation from someone else." Yet, the victim role blames the failure of their relationships on their sexual orientation. Seldom are the difficulties of lesbian relationships seen in terms of the realities of mainstream female conditioning in our culture and its distrust of women's self-assessment or the assessment of women by other women.

Internalization of the blaming of one's sexual orientation for problems in relationships is the reason gay men, lesbians, and bisexual and transgendered people need an additional layer of psychological healing. This layer is not related to their sexual orientation, but to society's conditioning about the victim role. So, they must first reject mentally and emotionally the messages of the dominant society that blame their sexual orientation for anything negative. They must detach their psychological issues from their sexual orientation, never again blaming their sexual orientation for anything that they consider "wrong" about them and their lifestyles. But the system does not want them to do this for that would be stepping out of a major part of the victim role.

THEN THERE'S DENIAL

Instead of facing these issues and talking about them, there is often a deep denial about these feelings of hurt and inadequacy within gay communities. It is as if these issues are long past. Yet, they continue to be lived out on other members of the communities through suspicion and lack of trust. They continue to disrupt the most intimate same-sex relationships.

Professor Michael Warner in *The Trouble with Normal* argues that much of mainstream gay politics today is motivated by both a general cultural shame over sexuality and a specific unhealed shame among gay people over their sexuality. That's why, he writes, that hiding same-sex sexuality and denying that it is as important to people who are homosexual or bisexual as it is to people who are heterosexual, has fed a conservative element in national gay leadership. What he is arguing is that the search for "normalcy" and the privatization of gay sexuality as a means to acceptance and assimilation is a desire to look as "straight" as possible. The accompanying "politics of shame" which he defines is actually a capitulation to living what I am calling the straight role in all of its restricted manner, particularly around sex.

"I don't want to be defined by my sexual orientation," in many cases is a means of putting one's sexuality in the closet away from the sight of the world so as to be acceptable to the straight role. Yet, this desire to look straight publicly is the internalization of what the "straight" role says gay people are, and the internalization of the belief that their sexuality should not be public. The result is a desire to make same-sex sexuality hidden in order for gay people to become acceptable. This does nothing to challenge the inhumanity of the straight role itself. It does not challenge people who are heterosexual by orientation to face their own conditioning. It hopes to end oppression but not homophobia and gender roles.

Denial that this need for "normalcy" arises out of the unhealed nature of the victim role into which gay people are conditioned appears to be the case among some of the "out and proud" role models who try to set the direction for gay communities, particularly on the national level. Gay communities need human beings who break out of the "professional" look of perfectionism defined by a straight society. They need people who tell them what they themselves have gone through and what their heart-felt issues and struggles still are. Instead, members of gay communities see leaders who communicate to the rest of us that they have solved their problems, have ended the internalized oppression, and thus are healed. The leaders may even be counseling other gay people to take on the "straight role" in ways both Warner and national gay liberation advocate Urvashi Vaid have noted.

To the posturing of these leaders as moral authorities who counsel that gay people change to fit in, everyday gay people react as victims. These leaders, we feel, are so far "ahead" that they could not be like us. Their having-made-it-"out" otherness touches our victim role so that we may feel we should hide in shame. Like many women who look up to the few women who seem to have made it in a male-dominated culture, we believe these leaders must be different from us. They are heroes who have what we don't have, that right stuff again. And when they scold us to "get with it," like preachers and moralists, we back away further.

Competition among leaders for followers, attention, and acceptance both from the gay and straight communities, instead of attempts to build effective coalitions, covers deep personal hurts and needs within gay communities. That is why leadership disputes and conflicts are as rampant in gay communities as they are in the communities of any victimized group. This competition for attention and recognition rises directly out of the victim role in a capitalist society with its teachings that, like other commodities, there is not enough attention, love, power, and followers to go around. Such leaders often need their followers more than the followers need these types of leaders.

There are numerous ways to cover-up or deny self-hate. Activism has often been an old standby. But all of the means the system promotes to cope rather than to heal are available

— from work to alcohol, from drugs to sex, from hiding in home remodeling projects to club-hopping, from anger and bitterness to internalized homophobia and suicide, from the activism that leads to burn-out to the capitulation of conformity to the roles' stereotypes. Most studies show high incidents of addictions in victimized groups, especially among gay, lesbian, bisexual, and transgendered people. One cites the rate of addictions as ten times higher in gay men, lesbians, and bisexual and transgendered people than among "straight" people. Real cultural victimization is the reason for this high incidence of the use of coping mechanisms, but the victim role is the excuse for continuing to use them.

The verbal expression of the content of this self-hatred is the lists people construct of what they hate about the people of the group with which they identify. When gay men talk of what is wrong with gay men, they are talking about their own personal issues. "All they are interested in is sex" says nothing about sexual orientation and a lot about gender conditioning. Blaming it on one's essential orientation means that the one who speaks it has the same "flaw" which he must overcome, if he can. When women speak about what they don't like about women, they are accepting that the "flaw" is in their own womanhood, not the realities of gender conditioning.

The most common expression of this self-hate among non-heterosexuals is the feeling, often expressed as an argument for equal rights, that "I wouldn't choose to be gay if I had a choice." One can hear the sadness in this response when gay people say: "With all of the oppression, prejudice, hate, abuse, death, and self-doubt that comes upon gay people, why would I choose this life?" Here is a clear example of victimization installing the victim role. I'd do anything to stop the pain, they conclude, even being someone I am not, if I only could. No matter how true it is that sexual orientation is not a choice, this reaction reflects the self-hate of the victim role installed through the real past victimization.

Such an argument may be based on the best scientific and experiential evidence. Sexual orientation is not a choice. It may also temporarily be useful as a political strategy. It has brought some straight allies into the fold. But in the long run it plays into the victimization.

First, it takes the "straight" role, not merely a heterosexual orientation, as the model for life. It is the straight role that is affirmed with all of its obvious systemic conditioning about manhood and womanhood. Heterosexual people who step out of the role are also treated the way non-heterosexual people are. But whether it is the role or the orientation that one desires, saying "I would not choose, but can't help it" does not begin with arguments that affirm the worth and value of non-heterosexual human beings or any people that step out of the "straight' role that is acted out against non-heterosexual people. It merely speaks as if gay people are powerless victims.

Second, this argument colludes with the false assumption that non-heterosexual is a deviation from a human norm. It is arguing that gay people should be forgiven, put up with, tolerated, and maybe even accepted, for this deviation, disability, or flaw because they could not help it. It in no way changes or challenges the standard of judgment involved. Gay people were born with this fault and, the poor things, can't help it. They are flawed victims of life's game of chance, "biological errors."

Third, it assumes that if there were an authentically free choice, people would choose the straight role or even heterosexuality. There is no evidence for this because there is nothing about our society that would enable the free choice of heterosexuality. Heterosexuality and the straight role are enforced by fear and terror at every turn. Some writers have even called this "compulsory heterosexuality." As discussed in previous chapters, the straight role is not a free human choice but a dysfunctional, fear-based survival mechanism whose goal is to maintain the system and its gender conditioning the way it is.

The response that "we couldn't help it" enforces the systematically conditioned straight role. It does not begin with the non-victim stance that sexual orientation, including homosexual and bisexual orientations, are "gifts," "natural," meant to be, or God-given if that is the language one prefers. If we step out of victim role thinking, the only reason to end gay oppression and heterosexism is that love should be honored wherever it is found and however ineloquently it might be expressed in order to counter the fear-based nature of society and its conditioning. The real issue should be love, not fear.

BELIEVING THE SYSTEM

The victim role also internalizes as true the reasons the system gives for the actual victimization. It fails to see that these "reasons" are merely the system's excuses for justifying the oppression. There are always other reasons for prejudice and oppression than those that are spoken out loud. There are real reasons, and they are reasons which benefit the system.

People who are being victimized by oppression are supposed to believe at a deep level that the reasons society gives for their victimization are true. So, the victim role of white racism teaches people of color to believe that they are oppressed because there is some truth to the dominant group's prejudicial stereotypes of them. They are inherently inferior, mentally weak, culturally lacking, from inferior families, or lazy. They are supposed to believe that if people of color would change something about themselves, their oppression would end. And many people of color believe this and put their sole hope in how they must change and conform without confronting the larger systemic, institutional functions of racism.

For non-heterosexual people, the victim role conditions them to believe that they are oppressed because of their sexual orientation or the sex of people to whom they are attracted. Yet, as we have seen, from the beginning this is the system's excuse for the oppression, while the oppression of transgendered and bisexual people, gay men and lesbians actually is an important means of installing, maintaining, and enforcing restrictive gender roles. It has nothing to do with sexual orientation and a lot to do with a cultural sickness about gender definitions which puts all people out of touch with their full, inborn humanity. In our culture the oppression of gay people functions to protect everyone from the need to face their fears about redefining who they are at a basic level. It protects everyone from their fears about changing the cultural institutions themselves. Stepping out of the victim role is saying with conviction and assurance in opposition to the dominant teachings that, "It is not me. The culture is crazy-making."

So, if the victim role is fully internalized, the victimized person believes that she or he deserves the oppression received. And they are convinced that they receive it because of something about themself, when in actuality this system requires the oppression and its scape-goats for it to survive. The false belief of the gay victim role is:

- if one were more masculine or more feminine,
- if one used different mannerisms and actions,
- if one were more disciplined,
- if one didn't look the way one does look,
- if one were smarter,
- if one were richer,
- if one didn't let people know that one thinks about sex as much as straight people,
- if one could get married,

— in other words, if a gay person lived the straight role better — then, the oppression would change. In addition, the belief says that it is one's own fault for not being the way the straight role says one should be.

NEEDING STRAIGHT APPROVAL

Another mark of the victim role is that it values the opinions and approval of those in the dominant categories more than the opinions and approval of those in one's own victim group. A book or article by a gay, lesbian, bisexual, or transgendered person is taken to have less authority or weight than that of a straight ally. The victim role believes, as does the straight world which teaches it to the victim, that gay people who write about sexual orientation are less objective than straight people.

I remember recommending John Boswell's classic work on early attitudes toward gay people, *Christianity, Social Tolerance and Homosexuality*, to a Christian minister. His first reaction was to ask if the author were gay. I could not let this pass and said, "I know why you are asking that. You are afraid that if the author is straight, he will skew the evidence to maintain the superiority and privileges of heterosexuality." Of course, that was just the opposite of his interest in the answer, but he got the point.

People in the conditioned victim role are taught to do the same as people in the straight role. The conditioning says that those in the dominant role are objective, as if they have no personal stake in the matter and no axes to grind. But gay people are too personally involved to write objectively. Gay people are prejudiced, not straight people. Unfortunately, too many gay people believe this.

In part this preference for straight opinions is due to the victim role conditioning gay, lesbian, bisexual, and transgendered people to emotionally need the approval of those in the oppressor groups before they feel good and acceptable about themselves. Gay people do not want to admit this so blatantly, but it is understandable. Straight people have the power in most circumstances to reject or gain acceptance for gay people in the institutions of our society. They dominate them.

Even more crucial, all of us were surrounded by "straight"

people in our formative years, people who gave us negative messages about non-heterosexual orientations. Like every child, we each desperately needed and wanted the approval and support of our parents and other adults.

As adults we can continue to live out that desperate need for approval and validation, and we often do. It is standard victim role conditioning to value the approval of the dominant group more than approval from one's own group. But this is to devalue the approval of someone with a similar sexual orientation on the basis of the orientation itself. Since it is also the orientation we share, to devalue people of one's own orientation evidences devaluation of self-approval as well. Ultimately, then, we are facing the psychologically unhealthy stance of not being able to embrace fully the ultimate value of self-worth.

Gay people lecture each other about the importance of making pride festivals and parades look good for "straights." Get rid of the drag queens, the radical fairies, and the leather men, they say; in other words eliminate anyone who doesn't look straight enough. Then we'll get their approval. But are they sure?

Gay people speak negatively of "gay" institutions. "We don't want to go to a gay church," for example. On the one hand this can merely mean a church without heterosexual people, but often with further examination there is more to the word "gay" in such criticisms than the issue of sexual orientation. There is something else about such a church gay people themselves don't like, and that something else is here tied to their own sexual orientation.

This need for straight approval causes those in the victim role to miss the dynamics which are actually playing out in criticisms from straight people. It also maintains prejudices and "straight" dominance.

A major daily newspaper printed a feature article entitled "She's Straight, He's Not." Building on the popularity of a current, prime-time television show, entitled "Will and Grace," where a straight woman is best friends with a gay man, the reporter interviewed gay men who were close friends with heterosexual women.

I was one of those interviewed. I talked about such relationships as a new model for interaction between the sexes, a model which could break old gender conditioned patterns for love and friendship. So did my good friend, who told me later that as she was interviewed the reporter seemed to have "no clue about what she was saying."

The published article centered around two analyses of these relationships. In true gender conditioned fashion, the reporter indicated regular disbelief that these relationships could not be sexual. There must, she concluded, be something wrong. Then, to explain these relationships she sought the opinion of a psychologist who reduced them to men trying to relate to their mothers, as if straight relationships did not find men seeking a mother figure. The result was an article that saw another type of relationship involving gay people either as psychologically unhealthy or in denial — not an unusual way for the dominant media to portray gay relationships.

Yet few of my gay acquaintances saw this. They told me how good the article was. When I indicated that I objected to its presentation on the above basis, they replied that they were just glad the newspaper did something about gay people.

Settling for what activist and analyst Urvashi Vaid has extensively documented to be "virtual equality" in her book by that name is settling only for what those in the dominant role allow victims to have. And that is ultimately dis-empowering. It is fitting in, conforming, and capitulating. It is settling for standards set by the "straight" role, not those in touch with anyone's freely chosen and unconditioned humanity.

EXPRESSING POWERLESSNESS

The powerlessness inherent in the victim role can be expressed as well in anger or blaming. It shows itself when people get stuck rehearsing the content of the oppression through anger against "the right wing," "men," "the rich," or whomever the oppressors are. It shows itself in the reactions of gay people who regularly watch television evangelists and political leaders whom they know abuse them. It gets them angry again, as if, after all this time, they thought it wouldn't! They may even find such abuse in some sense entertaining, while psychologically it also provides more data to validate life in the victim role. Complaining and blaming are the acting out of the victim role's sense of powerlessness.

This again is not to deny the reality of the sense of injustice behind the anger of those who have been victimized, the reality of past and present oppression, nor the need to know one's enemy. It does not mean that anger should not be fully acknowledged, fully felt, and fully experienced. People who are oppressed get angry. What a surprise that they don't always like their oppressors or that they don't act with kindness in return! And politically one should know the latest tactics of one's abusers.

Yet a continual repetition of the anger, the continual return to the abuse, is a debilitating rehearsal of a pattern of powerlessness and even self-abuse which can be addictive in itself. It is acting out the belief that *they* have to change before *I* will or before *I* can live my life. It is not doing what it takes to make my life safe.

Waiting for "them" to change is counter-productive and ineffective. It is settling for the personal psychological position that one's life depends on *their* attitudes.

Gay people know what could happen to them if they should hold hands in public, but at some point they have to decide if living a life never doing so is worth it. Fear of criticism or "what others think" needs to be faced. In addition, not living one's life openly allows the system to grind on. People never get to see the alternative to the straight role. It protects others from *their* feelings, from dealing with *their* part of homophobia and oppression. But personally it is also living in the victim role.

The victim role even gets one stuck rehearsing the real offenses and acts of oppression that have taken place. Going over again and again what happened is important in therapeutic settings where the feelings themselves can be accessed and expressed in a healing manner so the old feelings lessen and lose their power. But the continual repetition of the offenses without evidence of progress in the discussion is getting stuck in the victim role.

In contrast, rejecting the victim role includes in all such discussions a strategizing about solutions. It rejects the role through healthy, empowering responses such as: What are we going to do to end what is hurting us? How can we lead and organize to change things? Or, what's our next step to do so? This move to determine "what we can do" takes back one's sense that we have alternatives and that there is something that we ourselves can do about it. It affirms that those who have been victimized in the past are not helpless, but have the ability, power, and resources to do something for themselves. This is the outward movement to change things that contradicts any conditioned role. It stands up against everything that would condition any of us into hopelessness.

Victim groups cannot wait around for those conditioned to be in the oppressor group to finally "get it" and stop the oppression. There is no historical evidence that such waiting ever ended discrimination and oppression. Yet, victim groups fear that the dominant groups will abandon them or use any of the other means for enforcing the victim role such as violence, threats, ridicule, and humiliation. That's why some leaders counsel that the time is not right, that "straight" people should be given more space to change, that you shouldn't "push" them, or you should be more understanding and less demanding. Waiting around for others to change before one takes complete charge of changing what hurts one's own life, reflects again the dis-empowerment of the victim role.

VICTIMIZING OTHER VICTIMS

Victim groups know the further victimization that can come down upon them if they act out the content (their unhealed past pain and hurt) of the victim role on oppressor groups. Therefore they tend to act out their pain where they are less likely to receive more victimization. They promote or collude with the oppression of others whom the system has victimized.

One would expect that civil disturbances in south Los Angeles would pit people of color against each other, African-Americans against Asian-American shop owners for example. One would expect that white racism would act itself out in "Black on Black" crime. One would also expect that those in minority communities would blame themselves for their problems or give up on their communities and not focus on the white racism. That would fit the victim role.

The victim role looks for those who are even further victimized to discriminate against. Any group of men from a victim group acting out oppression of women or children is acting out the victim role.

When gay males promote discrimination against women and lesbians through lesbian jokes and putdowns, through criticisms and jokes of "women's stuff," through lack of support for women's issues, they are acting out their own victimization on women. Instead of working to change the total system that ultimately is responsible for their own oppression, instead of challenging the gender roles which maintain homophobia and heterosexism, instead of dealing with their own hurts around how some individual women have treated them, it is easier to join the putting down.

Any group of people acting out oppression on younger people, such as teenagers, is acting out the victim role. Blaming them, putting them down, shunting them aside, and treating them as less than full human beings has been a means for adults not to take up their own issues and examine the insecurities young people raise in adults. Journalist Mike Males, whose most recent book on this topic is *Framing Youth: 10 Myths About the Next Generation*, has documented the political strategies behind these national and cultural anti-youth attitudes and actions. Yet within any victim group, young people are often devalued and marginalized as a lost group of worthless party people who are somehow less valuable, less moral, less insightful, and less serious than older generations.

In fact, the separation of older and younger generations through either group stereotyping and putting down the other, effectively cuts victim groups off from knowing their histories. Without hearing the stories and knowing the real human histories of how things have changed and where they haven't, further progress seems impossible, current challenges seem insurmountable, and hopelessness and a conservative protectionism seem like the most rational response.

Gay male and lesbian oppression of people identified as bisexual or transgendered is acting out of the victim role. The issue of gender identity and definition that the transgendered embody is central to the acceptance of all non-heterosexual people, as we have seen. But the ambiguity of those who are bisexual and transgendered raises issues in gay men and lesbians that reflect their own victimization for not being "straight." We all fear the ambiguous. It challenges our settled dichotomous patterns of thinking — male or female, gay or straight.

Even acting out an oppressor role through jokes, slurs and names towards heterosexual people who are conditioned into the straight role, is not living as a full human being but the action of the victim role. Criticisms of heterosexual people sound more like reactions out of the hurts of non-heterosexual people than healthy decisions to change the system that effects us all.

Often upper class or professional class victims oppress working class, or rural victims. Those who have "made it" in some sense in the system pass down the victimization by labeling others in their own group as "lazy," "untalented," or "hopeless," as if the problem were the people, not the system. Gay men who move in high political or financial circles are the most likely to believe that they are not like those others and that those others should just (note the conditioned male sound of the following) "get over it, be responsible, get to work, stop whining." Lesbians might do this as well, but they seem less likely to do so when they understand what sexism did to them. Those who have made it forget how tokenism works — it allows a few, but never the majority, to get through, so that the system can deny that any systemic oppression exists.

National, glossy, gay magazines, like "straight" magazines, depend for their livelihood on the advertising that demands conspicuous consumption. They promote the image that the ideal gay couple is professional class, male, urban or lily white suburban, white, "successful," uninterested in sex, and up-to-date consumers who have their condominium or town home fully appointed with all of the latest electronic equipment and household amenities right down to the perfectly matching napkin holders on the always set dining room table. This couple drinks "good" wine and eats "good" food. They eat out regularly at the "finest" restaurants and drive the "best" cars. They listen to music that has "class," buy the latest gay clothes, attend concerts and the opera as often as possible, and appreciate "good" art. Since "good," "finest," "best," and "class" are defined in terms of money — rich people are willing to pay a lot for them, such an image of the ideal gay person betrays the ever-present class issues of U.S. society as acted out in the victim role.

Yet most people in this country are not an effective part of the owning class — at most they own only a portion of their residence. They are members of the working class, though they often prefer to think of themselves as "middle class." This means that any movement that is not classist will find most of its images among working class people. But of all oppressed groups, gay men have worked hard to reject that working class image and may even put down those who do not.

STEREOTYPING, COMPETING, AND CRITICIZING

The victim role can also be lived by mimicking the oppressor role itself to exaggeration, often developing it as an armor against further hurts. Gym culture, business culture, beauty culture, perfect relationship culture, all provide armor to protect one from further hurt. Looking these parts can be more than play-acting. Gay people can really start to believe that it works. Of course, living the "straight" role even with a homosexual orientation, is the goal of the system, but doing so is not living as a human being outside the conditioning. The straight role is definitely rewarded. Living it to exaggeration is a way to deny oneself and affirm the role's value.

Living the victim role can mean defending the oppression's stereotypes of the victim group. It can hide the unique self each one is, by living an exaggerated version of the role; taking on characteristics of the role to identify with and be accepted by others in it. There has been too much criticism from those who value the straight role, of the fascinating variety of radical (non-straight) ways that gay people live to thoroughly analyze from a "non-straight" perspective how some of these may be exaggerations acting out the victim role. However, it is likely that this also is a part of the picture that the victim role paints.

It means believing the negative things said of the leaders and members of victimized groups by mainstream media without further evidence. Since the mainstream, corporate media have a long history of misrepresenting victimized groups and because they have a stake in maintaining the current system, suspicion of its coverage of gay events and gay leaders would be the first order of business. Yet the victim role assumes the worst, rather than assuming the best of those who step into leadership until they have personally given reasons for other interpretations. This internalized negative projection on leaders keeps groups divided so that they are less powerful against the system.

The victim role also promotes competition both within the victim group and with other victim groups to see who can be the best "victim." Victimized people are supposed to live the systemically defined role as well as possible for fear that worse will happen if they step out of the role. Living the victim role results in greater rewards from the system. Those gay people who thereby stay in their place, not "flaunting it," and not standing up against prejudice, are tolerated. They are supposed to criticize those who do not conform for "bringing trouble" onto the community.

The victim role often includes criticizing and attacking leaders of liberation movements, particularly outspoken or activist leaders, behind their backs through gossip and negative assumptions about them from other victims who remain comparatively hidden. Instead of personally meeting with the leaders to understand their positions, it assumes they have ulterior and sinister motives.

The victim role fosters arguments with victims of other oppressions that "my" victimization is worse than "theirs." Whether the oppressions aimed at people of color are better or worse than the oppression of gay men, lesbians, and bisexual or transgendered people, is difficult to judge objectively and actually irrelevant.

Such arguments arise out of the view that any attention to one group must be at the expense of one's own — a view that the system loves since it teaches that we are all vying for a limited amount of human resources such as attention, appreciation, encouragement, power, and love. And arguing over who's oppression is worse keeps people who have victimization by the current system in common, from working together to end what systematically oppresses everyone.

In summary, in the dynamics of gay oppression, gay, lesbian, bisexual and transgendered people are conditioned to live a role that maintains the system. The system needs gay people to live the victim role which in this chapter I am calling "gay."

Being the best victim means living as closely as possible to the role that "straight" society defines for non-heterosexual people and wants them to live. It means hiding one's sexuality, conforming to the gender roles, being silent about heterosexual privileges, and not causing trouble by coming out and being proud of it. It means doing well all that has been outlined above and criticizing those gay people who do not conform.

No one is inherently a victim and all people at times live in the role of a victim. Yet when gay people base any of their internal evaluation, life choices, sense of worth, and activities on the "straight" role and what it teaches about gay people, they are living the victim role. Whenever they feel they are hopeless, helpless, or powerless, the victim role is manifesting itself.

Having a non-heterosexual sexual orientation is not the deepest issue. The system must condition non-heterosexuals to live the "gay" role and enforce it on each other to keep the system going. Gay men, lesbians, and bisexual and transgendered people are conditioned to believe that somehow they are at fault.

On the one hand, it would be easy to deny that the role is the issue. It would be easy to live in such denial as if one were emotionally isolated above the role and the uncomfortable feelings involved.

And guilt and shame over the extent to which one has lived out the role are unproductive and immobilizing. Both make change more difficult. Both constitute further victimization of oneself. Both dis-empower the victimized individual and movements toward liberation. When embraced, both confirm to the "straight" world that gay people are exactly who "straight" people think they are.

On the other hand, the healing that enables our re-emergence as full human beings again requires us honestly to recognize when we live oppressor and victim roles. It then requires a commitment to define who we are for ourselves, as unconditioned human beings who connect with other human beings not as one role connecting to another role but as one human being to another human being, with all that it means to be human including our sexual orientation. It recognizes that this system can change. It knows that changing the system takes clarity and commitment. It understands that what is necessary is a commitment to one's own life so that one no longer is willing merely to settle and survive, but to grow and thrive individually and together. It takes a commitment to being human again.

FURTHER READING

Rob Eichberg, *Coming Out: An Act of Love*. New York: Plume, 1991.

Mike Males, *Framing Youth: 10 Myths About the Next Generation*. Monroe, ME: Common Courage Press, 1999.

Urvashi Vaid, *Virtual Equality: The Mainstreaming of Gay Liberation*. New York: Doubleday, 1996.

Michael Warner, *The Trouble with Normal: Sex, Politics, and the Ethics of Queer Life*. New York: The Free Press, 1999.

Mel White, *Stranger at the Gate: To Be Gay and Christian in America*. New York: Plume, 1995.

CHAPTER EIGHT

HOW TO BE HUMAN

Like it or not, these roles of male, female, straight, and gay were installed in us through cultural conditioning. No matter what our sexual orientation is, the system attempted to condition us into, and expects us to conform our lives to, these roles. But none of these roles is our destiny. They have been learned and they can be unlearned. In fact, we are probably already "negotiating" these roles in numerous ways in every interaction we have with others and even as we relate to ourselves.

Sometimes our personal negotiations are conscious — when we face ourselves in the mirror and know that we would be doing, or would have done, something quite different if we weren't so afraid of others' reactions or of society's consequences, such as a loss of income. Often these internal negotiations of the roles are unconscious and quite automatic because we have become convinced mentally and emotionally that our only viable alternative is to live elements of the role. All else looks like chaos, loss, lunacy, and loneliness.

All of us can merely cope with society around us by playing these roles. Like the alcohol and other substances of substance addictions, living the fear-based roles itself keeps us from feeling our emotions — particularly our fear of the consequences of stepping out of the roles. Even the activism which fights against these very roles can function as such an addiction. For all its good results, activism often turns our attention outward so as not to feel what is going on inside. And denial that we have ever been affected by the roles, or denial that we are still affected by them, can also keep us from doing the internal work that is part of returning ourselves to a free, unconditioned, self-chosen definition of humanity.

CHANGING MAPS

No matter what our sexual orientation and no matter what roles the system wants us to live, healing ourselves and our culture requires what many observers call a "paradigm shift," a dramatic change in the mental-emotional model, the view of reality, we use to interpret ourselves, our society, and the world around us. Author and motivational speaker Stephen Covey illustrates the nature of such a paradigm shift using the image of a map which I take a step or two further.

Imagine that I am to meet a good friend in Chicago. I have not been there before, so my friend sends me a map to locate his home. But the printer has made an error, and the map labeled "Chicago" is really a map of Detroit. After I land at Chicago's O'Hare airport, I pick up my rental car, take out the map, and drive. Very soon, I realize that I am thoroughly lost. So I find a payphone and call my friend. He tells me that what I need is to read the map more carefully, drive more efficiently, and watch street signs more closely. In other words, though what is wrong is my basic set of definitions about what is going on around me, he says I should change my behavior.

This is a typically systemic answer. The system does not want us to think its "map" is the problem. It wants us to focus instead on individual behavior. That's why we are taught that if we would only act differently, stay in the roles, and hide in the closet to look "straight" better, then we would be able to get along successfully.

So, lost in Chicago with a map of Detroit to navigate by, I take my friend's advice and change my behavior. I stop regularly to check the map. I drive faster. I top off the gas tank, have the oil changed, get a tune-up, and check the air pressure in the tires. But I am still lost because my map, the model of reality I have been given, is incorrect.

At another payphone I call my friend again. "Maybe you need a different attitude," he advises. When I read the street sign on the corner to give him my location, he says, "Look, there's a bookstore right down the block from your phone booth. Go in and buy some books on developing a more positive attitude."

Now attitude is important. However, a change in attitude which merely causes me to drive by the wrong map in a happier, more accepting, more optimistic fashion, a change which enables me to cope with the frustrations resulting from having the wrong map with a smile on my face, is not the solution to the basic problem.

The solution is a whole new map, a new paradigm, a new view of reality. The map we have been given does not work for us personally. Nonetheless, the roles we have been taught, their definitions of who we are supposed to be as male, female, straight, and gay, persist. At the same time, the societal institutions that make, sell, and distribute the map, use it to promote the reconstruction of Chicago in the image of Detroit so they do not have to give up the map itself and the profits, investments, and coping benefits the map provides to them.

Throwing out the old map and drawing our own map of the city from our own experiences in it would seem to be the healthy response and, in brief, that is what returning to our preconditioned humanity with its free life-choices is. It means giving up the conditioned roles, the prejudicial evaluations of ourselves and others they give us, the definitions of what is natural and unnatural, and the hierarchies of dominance. It means defining who we are for ourselves with the support of others, and defining how we want to live our humanity with other human beings.

The process of changing maps is not that easy. When it comes to the uninstalling of our conditioning, the reprogramming of the current definition of reality, we have seen that the map is not merely some piece of paper out there which we examine and ponder. It is more like software installed inside us not only through misinformation but through the emotion of fear. That's why the hardest work for us to do is not reeducating ourselves. It is not merely obtaining the data society did not give us because that information was not useful for maintaining the system, and might even undermine it all. It is not merely noticing the logical problems with this information and deciding no longer to accept those teachings.

That is all important, but because of the manner by which we were conditioned, the hardest work is internal and emotional. In the process of shifting paradigms, we are required to face the feelings that installed the software, to feel those emotions again, and to express them in an appropriate manner and a safe place until they have once and for all left us. This might require individual counseling, participating in groups that support one's healing beyond mere substance abuse issues, and creating friendships or other relationships where we can examine our past, get in touch with the emotions of the past, and express those emotions in a conscious manner.

We can make all of the excuses in the world. But no matter how much we may not want to do both, a paradigm shift, progressive change, and authentic healing have two inter-related movements which ultimately must be pursued simultaneously. First, one must do the personal healing from the past that is necessary. Second, one must work to end what is hurting all of us. The first is an inward journey. The second is outward and activist. Doing the first keeps one from acting the second out in a victim role or turning activism into an addiction that ends in bitterness, denial, and the burn-out that comes from basing one's being on the success of one's activism.

Those for whom activism is easy need to focus on the first for themselves and their activism. Those for whom the internal journey is a safe place must not hide there, but for their own healing need to take up the second. And they must not wait until they have perfected the internal journey but take up the active path soon. One can't merely put salve on a burn from the stove and let the stove continue to burn one's arm. But merely turning off the stove does not heal a wound successfully. It leaves an open wound or at best a scar that will call attention to itself almost every time one stretches out an arm to turn off another burner. The non-attended wound's painful memory is not left in the past but reappears even in later preventative activities.

Let's admit that we are all in need of healing, both psychologically and sociologically, in spite of the fact that we would like to believe otherwise. We not only have emotional wounds to open and cleanse. We also have institutions and attitudes that we need to change so that the conditioning we and future generations continue to receive, and which continues to enforce the roles on all of us, no longer has power over us. We need to replace this conditioning with new definitions, new processes, and humane institutions that affirm human beings without fear-based roles. We need a totally new internalized and external map.

To admit the pervasiveness of this common need and our part in it, is to recognize that our culture itself is sick and that, unless we are active in healing, we all enable that sickness to continue. Anne Wilson Schaef as an expert on addictions and the addictive process, concludes that our cultural system is itself an "addict." In books with titles such as *When Society*

Becomes an Addict and *The Addictive Organization*, she argues that the system as a whole as well as its individual institutions function like addicts.

Like any addict, then, the system needs us to be its "enablers." The alcoholic needs people around to enable and maintain the addiction by ignoring the addiction, covering up the addiction, creating myths about the addict and the addiction, making excuses for the addict and the addict's behavior including the addict's mistreatment of others, and blaming themselves for the addict's problems. Just so, our society also needs us to do the same thing for it.

In Schaef's work, workshops, and writing, she joins other "recovering psychotherapists" who boldly break from the psychotherapy that holds that we merely need to change our personal behaviors and attitudes so as to fit in, assimilate to, and cope "successfully" with the system. She names the system as the central problem. She concludes that it would be hard to find anyone brought up in this system who was not affected enough by it to possess their own coping mechanisms. These coping mechanisms may be what society usually labels addictions or they may be the roles we are conditioned to fulfill.

THE INTERNAL JOURNEY

As "enablers," then, the first step in the personal and internal movement of our journey to recovering our humanity is to break through our own denial. Most people seem to find it easier to deny the depth of the effects of the conditioning on themselves individually than to face the feelings that need to be addressed. They are like the person who says "my parents hit me regularly and I turned out all right," alcoholics who blatantly deny their habit in the face of everyone around for whom it is obvious that they have a drinking problem, or those who joke about being workaholics and continue on at the expense of their closest relationships as if workaholism too isn't a fatal disease. It is so much easier to believe that the effects of past hurts and conditioning are behind us, done, finished, or other people's issues, than to live conscious of the emotions that we have tried so hard to live without feeling, as if perhaps we can live above them.

Some common denial mechanisms of those conditioned into an oppressor role are:

- denial that there is any problem at all,
- denial that something does hurt, or should hurt, the victim,
- denial that any of the hurts the victim identifies are other than the victim's own fault (their inferior talents, genes, family structure, behavior, effort, or attitude),
- denial that the oppressor is really hurting someone,
- and denial that they mean to be hurting someone.

These are strikingly similar to the denials of the spouse abuser.

Some common denial mechanisms of someone conditioned into the victim role are:

- denial that they have been hurt in the past,
- denial that there are any hurts from the oppression remaining to be faced in the present,
- denial that the system really meant to hurt them,
- denial that anything should have hurt them,
- and denial that the hurt is anything other than their own fault.

These parallel the denials of the abused spouse who refuses to leave the abuser. Both sets of denials must be faced, named, and rejected.

The second step inward is to accept that our systemic conditioning needs healing. The events that installed the systemic roles are hurts much like the incidents related to personal childhood hurts from dysfunctional family systems. John Bradshaw, the family systems specialist and popular writer, has come to address more the place of systemic issues in his recent writing, speeches, and workshops. He labels the broader problem behind our dysfunctional, individual family systems "patriarchy." This he defines as the current cultural system where masculinity in the form I have identified as "straight" is the dominant pattern.

Like family issues, systemic conditioning also begins in early infancy, as we have seen. It began before human beings had self-sufficiency, access to alternative information, and recognition that adults weren't always right. As children, we relied even more on the authorities and others from whom we needed love, sustenance, attention, assistance in processing and healing our hurts, and other elements needed merely to survive. Thus, our very existence depended on them to be right.

Author and psychotherapist Jean Jenson in *Reclaiming Your Life* explains the dynamics of these early hurts, the blocks to successful, complete, final processing of their pain, disappointment, and grief, and their consequent storage within, buried just below the surface. She also delineates a method for healing. What works for individual hurts and abuse works also for the fearful experiences that installed systemic conditioning. It requires the retrieval of the stored feeling-memories to bring them back to consciousness where they can be reexamined and dealt with head on.

The recognition within movements such as the "adult child" and "co-dependent" movements, that childhood pain must be felt as part of personal healing applies also to the process of effective personal healing from systemic conditioning. The feelings that installed the roles must also be felt and processed, or they will remain within to fester and appear again and again in the roles we are given or in our disproportionate and ineffective defensive reactions to the roles.

The third step in the internal journey is to engage the process that heals these wounds. As we look back to find those experiences and feelings that helped to install the roles that we are conditioned to live, we remember that they involved emotions and accompanying protective reactions to prevent violence, threats of violence, ridicule, humiliation, isolation, and rejection. We personally experienced these sanctions or took evasive action to prevent them from coming at us. We also saw that others were receiving this treatment because they were perceived to be outside the limits set by the roles of straight, and male and female. Though we may have buried these past events and their accompanying images, they remain within, effecting our responses to all the current events and images which trigger feelings from our past. We still carry and use the defensive mechanisms we used as children to cope and survive in the system, though these mechanisms may take more sophisticated "adult" forms.

Understanding these past experiences is good but not enough. Figuring them out, trying to theorize about why they happened, intellectually examining past experiences, and making sense of them are insufficient. As a total program for dealing with the past, intellectual analysis is actually an effective way not to feel our past emotions. Understanding and analysis do not deal with the anger, fear, hurt, and confusion that installed the conditioned patterns we were to live.

Schaef is adamantly opposed to settling for intellectual understanding alone. She goes so far as to say, "I have never seen anyone heal from understanding." Psychological "whys," she argues, function as one of the ways psychotherapy has perpetuated the system. Hiding in one's intellect is a way not to feel. And, as we have seen, moving to abstraction and analysis is a conditioned pattern, particularly for conditioned males, and thus a great support for the system that exalts the model of conditioned masculinity. Intellectual analysis alone functions to keep one out of touch with the primary feelings that installed the roles: fear, hurt, and confusion.

The recovery of the ability of each human being to affirm, recognize, and feel that full range of emotions, from anger to hurt, is so against the "straight" conditioning all have received, particularly males, that it seems difficult and, if we can admit it, frightening. As children, when we expressed emotions, whether they were considered appropriate or not by the conditioned paradigm, adults around us often reacted out of their own unhealed conditioning and usually did everything they had learned to do to stop the feelings. Operating out of their own backgrounds, they did what they thought and felt was best for us.

As children, we learned from this that there was something vulnerable, "wrong," and shameful about our feelings and about expressing them. We were never allowed to process fully and completely the hurts and fears that did not coincide with our unconditioned humanity, but which as children we knew had hurt. We may have been told that some of these things shouldn't hurt, or that we should just take them like an adult, like a man, or like a grown woman. We probably learned that we could even get hurt further for expressing the fact that we were hurt. We buried the facts and the feelings related to this conditioning which took much away from us and enforced much on us that we would not have freely chosen. When we were told, "boys don't do that" or "girls don't do that," or "boys don't feel that way" or "girls don't feel that way," we were denied what we felt, shamed for it, and separated from it.

It is no wonder that we might be in denial about this past and use every coping mechanism we can to deny that we were hurt and to not feel those feelings again. "Get over the past," we are told. And that is what feeling the emotions actually helps us do. Continuing to stuff them down within (the system-affirming answer) only serves to hide them so that we never get over them. It also supports the system by enabling the sale of remedies for dealing with the physical and psychological symptoms of these unexposed hurts.

These buried feelings fester within and often bubble up in disproportional reactions to the present. They eventually destroy us in depression, anger, bitterness, and burn out. And since the dominant teachings still do not want us to disrupt the system or do what will change it in any radical fashion, we receive the message over and over again that getting in touch with those past feelings is sick, disruptive, and dangerous. We may believe that if we were ever to express the rage and hurt within, those feelings would take us over and we would never get out of them. No matter how untrue those messages are, they seem powerful.

Two of the processes I use in workshops combating homophobia illustrate the beginning of this step. In groups of two or three people, I ask participants to take turns describing to each other two events from their pasts as best they can recall them. When it is not their turn, the others are to listen attentively without giving advice or attempting to "fix" the speaker.

One assignment is to describe in as much detail as possible an early memory and its feelings of when they were told, or in some other way received the message, that something they wanted to do or be was not appropriate to their gender. Memories related to families, religious institutions, schools, clubs, and camps usually come quite easily for the participants. Men sometimes tell of how they were discouraged from developing their artistic and musical interests, had certain toys taken away from them, and were forced into sports, highly competitive intellectual pursuits, or certain career tracks. Women remember being told something was not "lady-like" or "won't get you a husband," of the lonely life of the "old maid," of the need to "fix themselves up," or receiving the mixed messages about the possibility of being anything they wanted to be while also somewhere hearing that their goals as firefighters, scientists, or pilots were not normal.

One man told of how much he loved young children. From childhood on they were attracted to him and he was a gentle, nurturing presence who would babysit for neighbors and help out with the younger children at school. His dream in elementary school was that he would run a pre-school that would have a male adult presence. But many messages from many sources told him that this was not a manly occupation. One said that children need "a woman's touch." Another that it was not manly work. But the memory that most touched him was the day his father told him that men interested in little children must be sick. We should be suspicious of them. Instead, he should settle for teaching high school and maybe coaching.

This man, who became a nurturing father to his own three children, gave up his dream, depriving him of joy and many children of the love and care of a male who had not succumbed to the stifling male conditioning. Something had been taken from him. There was the sadness of a sense of loss in his words, which he recognized. That was the sadness he needed to feel again.

The second event they are asked to describe in detail is their first memory of when they learned what could happen to someone who was perceived to be gay or lesbian and how they felt at the time. It may have happened to them, or they may have seen it happening to others.

I remember vividly, for example, an experience at summer camp at that age of twelve where an overweight, fair-complected, unathletic boy (the way I picture "Piggy" in *Lord of the Flies*) was picked on mercilessly by the others, bullied by the more athletic boys, and accused of being a "fag." He received no protection from the counselors who seemed to be unaware, and was eventually hounded out of the camp. At twelve I did not stand up against the taunts and oppression because I did not want the same thing to happen to me. I remained silent in fear. Neither he, nor I, nor any of the other boys had an ally to help break the pattern, say the taunting was wrong, and stop the abuse. In that past event, the hurt was not happening to me directly, but it was happening to me as a part of that scene. I was learning the frightful consequences of not fitting the male gender role and of being thought of as gay.

The fourth step in the inward movement is the commitment to feel all our emotions. This is difficult for all of us, but imagine how difficult it is for men who need to appear "manly" in order to qualify as acceptable leaders. This commitment means we need to feel both the emotions of the present and those which relate to the past, particularly the emotions we are "not supposed to" feel. It means setting up safe and effective places to get in touch with and express rage, hurt, loss, abandonment, grief, and fear, as we remember the events that installed the conditioning. Often the events that installed the conditioned roles were tied to other events in our childhood that involve the personal traumas of dysfunctional families — a parent's alcoholism, depression, rage, incest issues, punishments, passive-aggressive methods, gender conditioning, absence, and death.

The commitment to feel our emotions does not mean acting out these feelings on the world about us, rehearsing the events again and again as if the people around us deserve to experience what is really from our past. That's what Schaef calls "pukeing out" the feelings on people. Instead, it means good, unpressured "deep process work" (Schaef's term) or "regression therapy" like that impressively detailed by Jean Jenson. I highly recommend Jenson's book, *Reclaiming Your Life*, for its practical, step-by-step, personal, and solution-oriented approach to the inward journey.

The places we set up to process our feelings are important, for as we experience our feelings in the world about us and during our activist work, we will have to put aside temporarily the expression of those emotions that arise. Those with whom we may be active in stopping what is hurting us, those who receive the benefits of our outward activities, and those who struggle along with us, may be the least able to give us the time and attention we need for our emotions. They may be too hurting, too caught up in their conditioning, and too in denial to turn their attention outward. We will have to "make a date with" the feelings to face them later. Then we will be with others who can give us the conscious, intentional attention we need so that we can return to feeling the past experiences that were triggered in our everyday life.

This means setting up individual friendships, partnerships, or communities of people who will listen carefully, pay close attention, refuse to judge us, and refuse to join us in our judging of ourselves. These partners in the journey are people committed to the idea that the expression of past emotions is a powerful act of healing, not a personal defect. They are committed to their own healing journey, believe in the fact that the attention they give heals, give no unsolicited advice, and do not have a psychological need to "fix" anyone. All of these attributes of such partnerships and support groups contradict the dominant "straight" paradigm and its conditioning. If we're well-conditioned, we'll fight against doing our inner work.

The inward journey then is not a short, brisk walk. It is a lifestyle which confronts all of the conditioning. The realization that this is a lifestyle change makes it seem difficult because so much appears to need changing in attitudes, definitions, and activities. Yet, that this change is not a single act but a commitment for a lifetime is what gives the journey its power. It is a life journey which requires a commitment to a life of healing. We do not expect to be "healed," whatever that means, because the journey is a process not a product, an exciting adventure not an outcome. It is measured by growth and process, not completion. One does not "get over it" by willing that to be so once and for all (a very conditioned male response). One commits to healing as a lifestyle. It is an adventure whose total journey is unique to every individual, but not an adventure to be done alone.

It is important that we are on this journey with others. There was some sense in which these traumatic past events took place in the midst of a past isolation. When we experienced these past events, there was usually no one else there with whom we could process the events and our emotions. We felt alone in these feelings without someone by our side to say, "Your feelings are just fine. The system is wrong." Had an ally been with us when we were learning through fear what we should or should not do or be, the feelings would have been processed back then and would be easier to deal with, or even non-existent, today. It is also likely that we received the message that we shouldn't even feel the way we were feeling. And the code of silence which fear installs seldom allowed anyone else to admit that they were feeling the same way. "Real boys" couldn't. "Real girls" couldn't. If they did admit that they were feeling the same, their respective manhood and femininity were in question and they could be treated the way gay men, lesbians, and bisexual and transgendered people are.

This is why the most effective healing requires breaking the isolation and processing our lives with others. It can be done alone, as Jenson shows, but setting up our own communities to do this is an important step out of isolation. The commitment to end all isolation and disconnection is the fifth step, then, but one not subsequent to step four, the commitment to feel all our emotions, past and present. Steps four and five go together. Both represent a further challenge to the systemic conditioning of the "straight" role.

The amazing fact is, that no matter how the system may try to bury the idea, we are not alone. There are many people out there who are on this journey at all different stages. When we feel that we are alone, we are feeling the old messages of past hurts — hopelessness, helplessness, and powerlessness.

The inward journey is a set of decisions. They are decisions to heal from the past, to allow no longer the past to dictate the present, and to contradict personally the conditioning around emotions, gender, and sexual orientation. Decisions made cognizant of, but not based upon, the feelings from the past are empowering and life-changing. They help us lead our own lives on our own terms in communities with others.

The progressive results of this internal work of healing include the following:

- clarity about what is actually happening to us and others at the present time;

- an ability to distinguish the present from the past including separating reactions and emotions hooked to past events from present emotions;

- an ability to choose, notice, and develop connections to others rather than isolation and distance;

- awareness of the present circumstances and conditions so as to effectively keep oneself safe and alert;

- the conscious choice at times to risk one's own physical comfort or safety for what one considers justice and love;

- the ability to take a relaxed interest in others even when they disagree and display their own lack of being in touch with their past systemic and personal hurts;

- the choice never to live the conditioned roles again;

- and the recognition that when we find ourselves returning to the roles or discovering new ways we are living the roles, we can remake the decision to leave them again without guilt, shame, or judgment for our need for further growth.

THE OUTWARD JOURNEY: BEING AN ACTIVIST

If we remain aware of our feelings, nothing will bring them up more than the second movement — being active in ending what is hurting all of us, stopping the conditioning of human beings through fear and terror into systemic roles. Ending the systemic hurting is the essence of activism. Its goal is to create something other than a fear-based system. Many spiritual leaders around the world have espoused this goal, going even further to replace a fear-based system with a love-based system. They envisioned a world without competition, fear-based teaching, oppressions, and macho posturing.

In setting out for outward change, we face numerous fears. "I'm not an activist type," people say. They look at the leaders of movements and see little in common with them. They see examples of confrontive activists in the streets and say "that's not my approach."

The system itself and its media portray activists as unusual people who are not like us common folk, or as disruptive, even evil, personalities. The media seldom help us understand the thinking, convictions, training, and strategies of activists, nor do they hold the system and its representatives responsible for the problems the media focus upon. The media emphasize the sensational or they sensationalize certain issues themselves, because that is what gets the most attention. They have little patience for examination of the systemic causes. The resulting portrayals of activists also isolate people from the possibility of thinking that they can change things in their own way and in their own backyard.

Since most of us have been brought up to respect "authorities," follow "role models," get love, respect, value, and support from others, find our meaning in the approval of others, "mind our manners," be nice and polite, offend no one, look pleasing, act like "ladies" and "gentlemen," and on and on, there are many messages that play into our feelings about not participating in activities which move toward ending the conditioning. In the end, what really makes us hesitate may be the fear that we will not get approval, benefits, and awards from others, especially those who have "made it" in the system. In fact, to stand up against the conditioning is to face the fear that those who stand up against it are liable to get the same treatment as those who are most victimized by it. It takes courage to stand up against what is hurting everyone.

The most important reason of all for challenging the feeling that one cannot be or "just is not" an "activist" is the fact that taking an outward stand, becoming active even in the smallest way, is a step of personal growth and healing. Only deciding to change one's own attitude toward the roles does not fully challenge the internal fear that keeps each of us in the "straight" role or the "gay" victim role. It is a beginning. But we still remain limited by the fear and self-hate that the roles install, and we manifest those limitations in our outer life by "fitting in" and "going along " with the conditioned "norm" about us.

We can personally choose, for example, no longer to tell jokes against or use slurs regarding gay people or anyone else who does not fit the "straight" role. But our fears dictate how we "act" when we are among others who do. Do we consent or collude with their words, attitudes, and actions in silence, thereby living and upholding an oppressor role? Or do we speak out, not requiring eloquent arguments, but merely responding with the observation that the joke or slur offends us as human beings, and with the conviction that the fact that it personally offends us is by itself the most worthwhile reason to stop it in our presence?

Those of us who are transgendered and bisexual people, lesbians, and gay men, can decide to no longer live a victim role, to no longer accept as valuable the "straight" role or all of the opinions and evaluations from "straight" people. We can decide to set up our own safety networks of people and connections that value and support us. We can choose to separate from those who refuse to let us live our lives on our terms. We can decide to challenge the norms and values of that "straight" role rather than judging ourselves by it and attempting to fit in even if our sexual orientation is not heterosexual. And we can set clear, empowering boundaries with those who object to our life of healing, letting them know how they will have to act if they want to be around us.

We can rethink and re-evaluate what we can and can't

accomplish for our lives in our workplaces, religious institutions, and families, and decide what we can do or what we are willing to give up of our lives in order to receive the rewards these institutions might give us. We will have to decide what institutions we choose to effect from within and which ones we would better leave. In essence, we have to step out of the victim role that is defined by the "straight role" and notice that those who are outside the role, because they stand outside it, have much to give to society to help it break out of its addictive process.

Bisexual and transgendered people, lesbians and gay men can lead in changing this fear-based society if they value themselves highly enough and they choose to do so. As spiritual writer Christian de la Huerta reminds us, gay people have filled the role of pioneers for numerous societies in the past. That's why he encourages them spiritually to step out of the victim role: "We have been holding on, holding back, playing small, hiding our light under a bushel. Enough of that. It is time to let go. We are needed now — all of us."

We may be afraid that others will see us as too "radical" and we may believe that "radical" (literally, "getting down to the root" of things) is a bad thing. We may be afraid that others will ridicule us with some other putdowns used for those who step out of the roles, such as "tree-huggers," "do-gooders," "bleeding hearts," "freaks" and even "queers." Those others, "gay" or "straight," may even separate from us emotionally and physically.

WORKING FOR OUR OWN HUMANITY

Even more personally debilitating is that we may believe from our past conditioning that our own voices are not powerful, important, worthy, expert, or strong enough. We may believe that the fact that we are personally offended by something someone says or does is not worthy of public recognition. As an individual, I may believe that the fact that something is offensive to me as a human being is not a strong enough argument for the offense to end. Like those I spoke of in the first chapter who take no responsibility for their own opinions and instead quote other authorities such as the Bible to give their prejudices validation, I may feel that my own stand is unworthy of consideration without relying on someone or something else for validation. So, I may decide to remain silent and stuck, a victim of my fears and feelings of unworthiness.

Outward actions are crucial because through them we break these patterns by contradicting the message that we are not capable, worthy, valuable, or powerful without the roles. Once we have taken such a stance, even in our own circles of friends and relatives, we have become "activists." We are now those who will be known for not tolerating what we believe offends all humanity and hurts everyone. The fears of ridicule and rejection this stance raises in us are those very ones we will bring up and process as progress on our inner journeys. And the combination of the inner and the outer will help us face what we ourselves must face to bring growth and personal healing to ourselves and others. Deciding to move outward is thereby a sign that we are ready to take an empowering and pro-active stand for ourselves, no longer limited by the fears that installed and maintain the conditioning.

In fact, this outward journey begins most effectively with the recognition that something is hurting ourselves. Self-interest is the most important and most effective reason to become active. It is also the most common. It is the reason most people who have brought or initiated change in the world became active. Though it may sound noble and highly religious to work to help "those people" who need "our help," ending the oppression of non-heterosexual people is best done when we see how their oppression effects us all.

Gay men, lesbians, and bisexual and transgendered people know their own stake in ending the oppression, and they have the power to do so. Ten percent of the population has proven to be more than enough historically to effect radical change. Their task is to step out of the victim role they are expected to live. But they are not the "heterosexual person's burden." They are not the "nice little people" whom those of us who are heterosexual must help.

Those of us who identify as heterosexual need to end the oppression of transgendered and bisexual people and lesbians and gay men so that we too can live free from the role of "straight" that limits and damages our lives, puts us out of touch with our unconditioned and freely chosen definitions of humanity, and keeps us in our fear. Understanding that our own lives and freedom are at stake and that we must end the oppression for ourselves, helps prevent the burnout that comes from depleting one's energies only for others at one's own expense. One then no longer needs to wait for the thanks of those others whom they are helping because one sees how the active life is changing one's own life and opening up new personal possibilities.

One organization with members who often see this clearly is PFLAG, Parents, Families, and Friends of Lesbians and Gays, an international organization which advocates for equal rights for, and full acceptance of, gay men, lesbians, and bisexual and transgendered people. The most common reasons people initially join PFLAG are either because a son, daughter, spouse, other relative, or friend has "come out" and it has become obvious that they are being mistreated, or because the new member needs personal support in dealing with a relative's or friend's disclosure, often by breaking out of the isolation one can feel in the light of the revelation.

Yet, as its members learn and confront their relative's and their own issues, they find that they too are changing. They see that they personally have a stake in gaining affirmation and equality for gay people. The issue becomes more and more personal, and they have a deeper cause for action. Even their views of reality and lifestyles change. As one participant responded to a homophobia workshop, "I thought I came to learn about someone else and left knowing much more about myself."

Just so, the nature and place of our activism begins where we are. At its best it is not asking what others need but what we need. Writer and teacher Parker Palmer understands this when he talks about living our "calling" (the root of the word "vocation," as opposed to merely having an "occupation" to *occupy* oneself), rather than merely doing what others need. Our outward journey to heal the world does not begin with what the world needs, because the world needs everything. It begins in a hurt, a cause, a place, and a process that changes us, touches us, makes sense to us, revitalizes us, and speaks to us — in his words, "in what brings the self joy, the deep knowing that we are here on earth to be the gifts that God created us."

Both history and the present overflow with examples of active, everyday people, men and women, professionals, laborers, people with occupations outside the home, and homemakers. They recognized that something was hurting them, their families, or their friends and organized, or became part of a movement, to stop it. Some eventually joined or organized even larger causes with national and international agenda. They began where they were with one project at a time. They never imagined that they had the talents or personality to do so, but they did, and they changed things and themselves.

Paul Rogat Loeb's recent book, *Soul of A Citizen: Living with Conviction in a Cynical Time*, is replete with examples of everyday people who decided to stop what was hurting them and were successful. Loeb discusses the perceptions, objections, fears, and insecurities which prevent people of conscience from taking action. I could recommend no better next book for anyone fearfully contemplating the outward movement on their journey to being human again.

Remember that what we were taught may have kept us believing that this outward movement is impossible, hopeless, and futile. If so we have been conned into believing that there are no healthy alternatives and that what we have is the best that can be. The system may need tinkering with here and there, but basically, we were told, we have arrived. This teaching instills hopelessness about any real change. As a feeling, hopelessness causes us to believe that nothing we do will work. It also substitutes for feeling other more primary emotions, such as fear, hurt, confusion, and anger which, unlike hopelessness, can motivate us to actively change things.

Near the end of a continuing education workshop I lead for social workers on understanding and working with men and their issues, I saw this hopelessness. As we came to the close of a day of hard theoretical and emotional work which they agreed was enlightening, they expressed the hopelessness of their profession. We were talking about what each had learned from the workshop and one man said, "But our job in working for the state is not to help people heal; it's to help them get along and cope with the system. We are supposed to get the troubled out of sight, keep the disruptive in their place so they don't disrupt anything, and make sure the system runs smoothly." We extended the discussion so that the thirty or so social workers could feel and begin to process together their dilemma — whether the system in which they worked would allow for real healing. They knew in their hearts that that is what they wanted. Now they needed to determine what to do about it either within the structures or by developing new structures including a support system for social workers who wanted things to change at the human level.

Just as it was for those social workers, even though things may seem hopeless to us, hope itself is a choice we make, a decision. If we feel isolated and alone in our desire to make a change, we will feel hopeless. By teaching us only the history of the dominant paradigm, our institutions have cut us off from the history of those who have worked for real change, against what would appear to be great odds. By determining that only the history of this dominant view is important and leaving out the history of the non-dominant, people of color, working class people, white women, and non-heterosexuals, they have cut us off from the vision that there is every reason for hope for real change. Even more insidious, they leave out the history of those "everyday" people who stood up and changed things, the dissenters and progressive activists who forced the powers to change.

Historian Howard Zinn has concluded after his extensive study of U.S. history, that progressive and radical change has actually more often than not taken place against systemic odds. It has also taken place because everyday people were tired of what hurt them and decided to lead and organize movements to end the hurt. In his own story as historian and activist, *You Can't Be Neutral on a Moving Train*, he concludes that history is actually full of hope, that power, however daunting it seems, is much more fragile than we think or feel, that ordinary people sooner or later find ways to challenge that power, that real, revolutionary change does not come through great, giant leaps, but in the "zig-zag" fashion of a succession of "surprises," and that the smallest of actions people take begins to multiply and transforms the world. ". . . No pitifully small picket line, no poorly attended meeting, no tossing out of an idea to an audience or even to an individual should be scorned as insignificant."

There is no question that there are humane alternatives to the roles that the system has convinced us are so real, so natural, and so necessary. Most of the time it may seem easier to conform to the roles. Unfortunately even the counsel of some gay, lesbian and bisexual leaders, often those who have "made it" in straight society, is not to challenge the roles but to fit in and assimilate as much as possible in order to relieve the oppression.

Some discrimination may end through the process of "fitting in," of conforming to "straight," but homophobia and the destructive "straight" role will continue. Gaining the right to marry, some counsel, is the solution, but the fact that people of color can marry has not done anything to end racism or to make the late twentieth-century image of the "traditional family" with all its "values" any less white.

Those of us who are transgendered, bisexual, lesbian, or gay have the opportunity to show all of us what lies beyond and outside the limiting roles the system has defined for us. These alternatives can help us return to our humanity again, but not if any of us keep them in the old closets or in a new one which is still "straight." And not if they themselves strive to conform to the straight role that is so rewarded in our system and therefore looks so tantalizing. Down deep we all feel, and even know, that "straight" is a lifestyle that is really our common straight jacket. We don't have to be "scared straight" any more. We can begin to free ourselves to explore alternatives that, since we left early childhood, we have rarely dreamed could exist.

Further Reading

John Bradshaw, *Creating Love: The Next Great Stage of Growth*. New York: Bantam, 1992.

Christian de la Huerta, *Coming Out Spiritually: The Next Step*. New York: Tarcher/Putnam, 1999.

Jean Jenson, *Reclaiming Your Life: A Step-by-Step Guide to Using Regression Therapy to Overcome the Effects of Childhood Abuse*. New York: Dutton, 1995.

Paul Kivel, *Men's Work: How to Stop the Violence that Tears Our Lives Apart*. New York: Balentine Books, 1992.

Paul Rogat Loeb, *Soul of a Citizen: Living with Conviction in a Cynical Time*. New York: St. Martin's Griffin, 1999.

Parker J. Palmer, *Let Your Life Speak: Listening for the Voice of Vocation*. San Francisco: Jossey-Bass, 2000.

Anne Wilson Schaef, *Beyond Therapy, Beyond Science: A New Model for Healing the Whole Person*. San Francisco: Harper, 1992.

Anne Wilson Schaef, *When Society Becomes an Addict*. San Francisco: Harper, 1987.

Howard Zinn, *You Can't Be Neutral on a Moving Train: A Personal History of Our Times*. Boston: Beacon Press, 1994.

ABOUT THE AUTHOR

Robert N. Minor, Ph.D. is Professor of Religious Studies at the University of Kansas where he has taught over twenty-four years and was Department Chair for six. His first five books were on his speciality, religious thought and practice in South Asia and their relationships to culture. His current research is on gender studies and the relationships of religion, gender, and sexuality. He writes a monthly column entitled "Minor Details" on issues affecting the gay community for *Liberty Press* (the Kansas state t/b/l/g magazine) and *Liberty Press Kansas City* (serving the greater Kansas City, Missouri metropolitan area).

At KU one of his popular courses is "Religious Perspectives on Selfhood and Sexuality." He is a single parent of a twenty-four year old son and in 1994 he was a member of the Values Panel for the *Kansas City Star* (the daily newspaper for Kansas City) for its nationally award-winning "Raising Kansas City Project." He was a member of the Communities Against Hate Crimes Task Force of the U.S. Attorney for the District of Kansas as well as other boards and task forces, such as the Diversity Advisory Committee of KCPT, the public television station for Kansas City, MO.

Dr. Minor leads workshops on gender roles, homophobia, and racism for universities, colleges, churches, government organizations, and community and religious groups throughout the U.S as well as workshops for non-heterosexuals on personal growth beyond "coming out." He is a regular conference presenter for PFLAG, locally, regionally, and nationally. In 1999 he received GLAAD's Leadership Award for Education.

Have a story, a reaction to this book, an idea, or a comment for the author? Send it to Minor@libertypress.net or visit www.fairnessproject.org.